Read! Perform! Learn!

10 Reader's Theater Programs for Literacy Enhancement

Toni Buzzeo

UpstartBooks

Fort Atkinson, Wisconsin

With thanks to my friend and editor Michelle who forged a wonderful partnership by greeting me on a Texas dais and inviting me to write for her.

Reader's Theater Permissions:

Page 10: Adapted from *Book! Book! Book!* by Deborah Bruss. An Arthur A. Levine Book published by Scholastic Press/Scholastic Inc. © 2001 by Deborah Bruss. Reprinted by permission.

Page 20: Adapted from *Chicken Soup by Heart* by Esther Hershenhorn, illustrated by Rosanne Litzinger. Text © 2002 by Esther Hershenhorn, Illustrations © 2002 by Rosanne Litzinger. Reprinted by permission of Simon & Schuster Books for Young Readers, an imprint of Simon & Schuster Children's Publishing Division. All rights reserved.

Page 33: Adapted from *Dinosnores* by Kelly DiPucchio. © 2005 by Kelly DiPucchio. Printed with permission of the author.

Page 44: Adapted from *Jingle Dancer* by Cynthia Leitich Smith. © 1996 Cynthia Leitich Smith. Reprinted by permission of Curtis Brown, Ltd.

Page 57: An adaptation of *Mudball.* © 2005 by Matt Tavares. Reproduced by permission of the publisher Candlewick Press, Inc., Cambridge, MA.

Page 70: Adapted from *Old Cricket* by Lisa Wheeler. © 2003 by Lisa Wheeler. Printed with permission of the author.

Page 83: Adapted from *Rain Romp* by Jane Kurtz. © 2002 Jane Kurtz. Reprinted by permission of Curtis Brown, Ltd.

Page 92: Adapted from *The Recess Queen* by Alexis O'Neill. Published by Scholastic Press/Scholastic Inc. © 2002 by Alexis O'Neill. Reprinted by permission.

Page 106: Adapted from *School Picture Day* by Lynn Plourde, illustrated by Thor Wickstrom. © 2002 by Lynn Plourde, text. Used by permission of Dutton Children's Books, A Member of Penguin Group (USA) Inc. All rights reserved.

Page 120: Adapted from *Violet's Music* by Angela Johnson, illustrated by Laura Huliska-Beith. © 2004 by Angela Johnson, text. Used by permission of Dial Books for Young Readers, A Member of Penguin Group (USA) Inc. All rights reserved.

———————————

Published by UpstartBooks
W5527 State Road 106
P.O. Box 800
Fort Atkinson, Wisconsin 53538-0800
1-800-448-4887

© Toni Buzzeo, 2006
Cover design: Debra Neu

The paper used in this publication meets the minimum requirements of American National Standard for Information Science — Permanence of Paper for Printed Library Material. ANSI/NISO Z39.48-1992.

Contents

Introduction 5
  How to Use This Book 5
  Preparation 5
  Using Reader's Theater 6
  Extending the Learning 6

Book! Book! Book! 7
  Meet Deborah Bruss 7
  Reader's Theater Script 10
  Activities 13

Chicken Soup by Heart 18
  Meet Esther Hershenhorn 18
  Reader's Theater Script 20
  Activities 25

Dinosnores 30
  Meet Kelly DiPucchio 30
  Reader's Theater Script 33
  Activities 36

Jingle Dancer 41
  Meet Cynthia Leitich Smith 41
  Reader's Theater Script 44
  Activities 48

Mudball 54
  Meet Matt Tavares 54
  Reader's Theater Script 57
  Activities 61

Old Cricket 67
  Meet Lisa Wheeler 67
  Reader's Theater Script 70
  Activities 75

Rain Romp 80
  Meet Jane Kurtz 80
  Reader's Theater Script 83
  Activities 86

The Recess Queen 90
  Meet Alexis O'Neill 90
  Reader's Theater Script 92
  Activities 96

School Picture Day 102
  Meet Lynn Plourde 102
  Reader's Theater Script 106
  Activities 112

Violet's Music 117
  Meet Angela Johnson 117
  Reader's Theater Script 120
  Activities 123

Introduction

Reader's theater is an exciting way to share literature with children and provide them with an opportunity to enjoy meaningful participation and effective reading practice simultaneously. What's more, reader's theater is a LOT of fun!

According to a study conducted by Dr. Carol Corcoran and A. Dia Davis published in *Reading Improvement* [1], "reader's theater is effective in improving student interest in reading, confidence in reading, and overall fluency in number of words read correctly per minute." It's really no wonder. Unlike the pressure of round robin reading where students might be expected to read aloud from unfamiliar text, reader's theater offers readers the opportunity to become familiar in advance with the text they will read, to practice it until they are fluent with it, and then to relish the positive experience of reading that well-practiced text aloud for an audience.

In a *Reading Teacher* article entitled "I Thought about It All Night," [2] Jo Worthy and Kathryn Prater tout the advantages of reader's theater for even challenged readers, noting that it "combines several effective research-based practices, but also leads to increased engagement with literacy even in very resistant readers." Worthy and Prater emphasize that with regular reading performances, "all students have the opportunity to practice, successfully perform, and increase their self-confidence." Those are three worthy goals!

Read! Perform! Learn! 10 Reader's Theater Programs for Literacy Enhancement is a resource for school library media specialists, public children's librarians, and classroom teachers who want to share excellent children's literature with their students while improving reading skills and extending the use of books into the content areas, meeting learning standards in English Language Arts and beyond.

How to Use This Book

Contents

In this book, you will find ten chapters, each devoted to one picture book. For each book, you will find an author interview, a reader's theater, and a set of standards-based learning activities with accompanying standards.

Preparation

Begin by reading the children's book you have chosen and the author interview yourself to become familiar with the story and its creator. Next, read the book aloud to students so that they can enjoy the illustrations and appreciate the nuances of the story as revealed through the art. Students will carry these visual images into their reader's theater experience. Finally, share the interview with students either by reading the questions and responses aloud to them (for older students) or by paraphrasing and sharing the information with younger students.

Using the Reader's Theater

Once you have read the script and matched students with parts—paying special attention to the level of challenge each part will pose for your various student readers—distribute a set of photocopied scripts to the readers. Ask the remaining children to be the audience. Allow readers to practice, providing as much support and advice as necessary to allow each child to deliver a successful reading.

Invite performers to face the audience and simply read their parts in turn on the first full cast run-through. Once all of the readers are comfortable with their parts, you are ready to stage a second reading with the opportunity to use props or costumes, if desired. Suggestions for each are provided in the introductory material for the script. You may also invite students to act out the story while reading.

Extending the Learning

Because literature can be a meaningful introduction to classroom or collaborative content area units or provide an extension of units under study, there is also

a set of standards-based learning activities for each of the ten featured books to accompany and extend student learning. Individual content area standards are drawn from the McREL document Content Knowledge: A Compendium of Standards and Benchmarks for K–12 Education, 4th Edition available at www.mcrel.org/standards-benchmarks/. In addition to English Language Arts activities, you will find activities for Science, Social Studies, Math, Art, Music, Physical Education, and Life Skills as well. I hope that these activities will help deepen your students' experience of the books while meeting content standards in several disciplines.

Most of all, however, I hope that you enjoy the books I have chosen, their talented authors, and the fun of sharing them through reader's theater with your students!

A Note about Web Sites: Because Web sites are constantly evolving, if you find a URL listed here that is no longer active, you might try performing a keyword search on the Web site title or domain name to locate the new URL.

---

1. Carol A. Corcoran and A. Dia Davis, "A Study of the Effects of Readers' Theater on Second and Third Grade Special Education Students' Fluency Growth," *Reading Improvement* 42, no. 2 (Summer2005):105–111.

2. Jo Worthy and Kathryn Prater, "'I thought about it all night': Readers Theatre for Reading Fluency and Motivation," *Reading Teacher* 56, no. 3 (November 2002): 294–297.

Book! Book! Book!

Read *Book! Book! Book!* and the interview with Deborah Bruss below to familiarize yourself with the book and the author. Once you are ready to perform the script with your students, read the book aloud to the children so that they can enjoy the humorous illustrations with their additional story line, as well as become familiar with the story. Then, hand out a set of photocopied scripts to 11 children. (Animal parts, except for the hen, are perfect for struggling readers.) Ask the remaining children to be the audience. Have performers face the audience and simply read their parts on the first run-through. Once all of the readers are comfortable with their parts, have a second reading with the opportunity to use props (three signs—Library, Farm, and Public Library—are a wonderful addition) or costumes, if desired, and to act out the story while reading. Note that, as in the book, the frog should be present throughout the reading, perhaps reading silently or looking at books. You might also consider asking all of the remaining children to be "frogs" throughout and to join in on the last line.

This book especially lends itself to animal masks. Try making paper plate animal masks. Simple instructions can be found at www.abc.net.au/creaturefeatures/make/masks.htm or enter the words "paper animal masks" into a search engine. You might also want a cow and librarian hand puppet, which, if you don't have them, are easily made by pinning a photograph to a glove.

Meet Deborah Bruss

Deborah Bruss did most of her growing up in rural New Hampshire and especially enjoyed wandering the woods on her pony, Echo. She wrote her first children's story while in college, but didn't take the idea seriously until after her two sons were born. When one of them struggled with reading, she wrote a story for him, which she later submitted to an editor and nearly had published. She then decided to take writing more seriously. For several years she

wrote for newspapers about the interesting things in her life—migrating salamanders, mud-loving children, and hungry porcupines (to name just a few). She continues to live in rural New Hampshire with her husband, two sons (when they are home from their travels), two daughters, and two of everything else: horses, dogs, and cats.

Book! Book! Book! is a story about libraries, reading, and books. Please talk about the role of each in your childhood.

DB: As a child, my favorite picture books were *Blueberries for Sal* and *Make Way for Ducklings*, both by Robert McCloskey. I was not a child who liked to sit down, so reading was not a big part of my life. I really fell in love with children's books when, as a teenager, I read to my little brother. The Paddington books got me laughing so hard that reading out loud was nearly impossible. Now I have four children. For years, reading to them was a favorite nightly ritual.

I am a children's librarian, and so I was very interested in the character of the librarian in Book! Book! Book! What is your personal connection to the librarian in the story, or do you have stories to share about the librarians in your life?

DB: After my two sons were born I went to work in a library at a very small elementary school with just eighty-five students. My favorite times in the library were: reading to the younger children and taking on the voices of the different characters; helping the students find books that interested them; and buying books for the library. Though I no longer work as a librarian,

I have several friends who are children's librarians. They are incredibly creative, and I wish that I could be in their classes.

An essential aspect of this charming story is the animal sounds, for it is the hen's "Book, Book, BOOK!" that finally grabs the librarian's attention and answers the animals' wish for something to do. Please talk about the creation of Book! Book! Book! Which came first, the story or the animal sounds?

DB: The story and the animal sounds came at the same time. My father had told me a joke about a chicken who knew how to ask a librarian for a book. I am not good at remembering jokes, but this one stuck with me. I knew it would make a wonderful children's story. The story developed from the joke. Every fall, when my children returned to school, our pets—dogs, pony, cats, and rabbits—became bored. I knew that the animals in *Book! Book! Book!* felt this way, too, and this is why they went to the library.

Traditionally, animal characters stand in for child characters in children's books. In Book! Book! Book! the reader meets a cast of animal characters including the horse, the cow, the goat, the pig, the duck, the bullfrog, and the hen. What were you like as a child? Were you the idea generator, sometimes overshadowed by larger children but ultimately triumphant, like the hen?

DB: I was always the smallest in my class, and still am shorter than most people I know. I was quiet when I was young but learned to speak up for myself as I got older. One of the ways I like to make my voice heard is through writing.

The collection of animals in this story forms a delightful team. How did you decide on these animals? Have they (or you) even considered another adventure for them off the farm?

DB: Since my son has a pony named Rhapsody-in-Blue there had to be a horse in the story. Tiphanie Beeke, the illustrator, did not know this when she created the pictures. I was quite surprised and happy to see a blue horse. As far as the other animals? A farm must have a cow. I think pigs are wonderful. (Who wouldn't after reading *Charlotte's Web*?) As a child I had a very stubborn goat. The duck just waddled her way into the story. The mouse was the wonderful creation of the illustrator.

These animals have gone on several other adventures, but none yet have made their way onto the pages of a picture book. I hope they will soon.

How can readers learn more about you and your writing?

DB: Readers can go to www.deborahbruss.com. Sign my guest book while you're there!

Book by Deborah Bruss

Book! Book! Book! illustrated by Tiphanie Beeke. Scholastic, 2001.

Book! Book! Book!

Narrator One:	Down at the farm, all was well until …
Narrator Two:	… the children went back to school and the animals had nothing to do.
Narrator Three:	They had no rides to share, no tug-of-war to play, no one to scratch behind their ears or ruffle their feathers.
Narrator One:	In the bright morning sun, the horse hung his head.
Horse:	**Neigh!**
Narrator Two:	The cow complained.
Cow:	**Moo!**
Narrator Three:	And the goat grumbled.
Goat:	**Baaah!**
Narrator One:	The pig pouted.
Pig:	**Oink!**
Narrator Two:	The duck dozed off.
Duck:	**Quack!** Zzzzzzz.
Narrator Three:	And the hen heaved a sigh.
Hen:	*(Sigh.)* **Book!**
Narrator One:	Long about noon, the sun was high above the barnyard.
Hen:	*(Squawk.)* I'm bored! And I'm heading to town to find something to do!
Narrator Two:	The animals followed her down the road.
Hen:	*(Cluck.)* Look! Happy faces. This must be the place we're looking for. I'll go in and see if I can find something to do.

Horse:	*(Whinny.)* **Neigh! Neigh!** You're too small for such a big job. Leave it to me.
Narrator Three:	The horse clip-clopped in.
Narrator One:	Politely he asked for something to do.
Narrator Two:	But the librarian could not understand the horse. All she heard was …
Horse:	**Neigh! Neigh!**
Narrator Three:	So the horse hung his head and clip-clopped out. Next the cow plodded in.
Narrator One:	Politely she asked for something to do.
Narrator Two:	But the librarian could not understand the cow. All she heard was …
Cow:	**Moo! Moo!**
Narrator Three:	So the cow complained and plodded out.
Narrator One:	Now it was the goat's turn, and *he* trotted in. Politely he asked for something to do.
Narrator Two:	But the librarian could not understand the goat. All she heard was …
Goat:	**Baaah! Baaah!**
Narrator Three:	So the goat grumbled and trotted out again.
Narrator One:	Slowly the pig ambled into the library. Politely she asked for something to do.
Narrator Two:	But all the librarian heard was …
Pig:	**Oink! Oink!**
Narrator Three:	So the pig ambled out to tell her friends.
Narrator One:	Up flapped the hen.
Hen:	I am going in, and no one is going to stop me!
Narrator Two:	Into the library she flapped.
Hen:	*(Cluck.)* **Book!**
Narrator Three:	The librarian looked around.
Librarian:	What's that noise?

Hen:	*(Cluck.)* **Book! BOOK!**
Narrator One:	The librarian scratched her head.
Librarian:	Who's that?
Hen:	*(Cluck.)* **Book! Book! BOOK!**
Librarian:	Oh! Is this what you want?
Narrator Two:	She handed the hen three books.
Narrator Three:	Back at the farm, the horse, the cow, the goat, the pig, the duck, and the hen gathered around the books.
Narrator One:	The barnyard was filled with sounds of delight that lasted until sundown.
Horse:	**Neigh! Neigh!**
Cow:	**Moo! Moo!**
Goat:	**Baaah! Baaah!**
Pig:	**Oink! Oink!**
Duck:	**Quack! Quack!**
Hen:	**Book! Book! BOOK!**
Narrator Two:	All the animals were happy, except …
Narrator Three:	… for the bullfrog. And do you know what he said?
Bullfrog:	I already **read it! Read it, read it, read it …**

The End

                          © 2006 by Toni Buzzeo (UpstartBooks)

Book! Book! Book! Activities

Social Studies Connections

Fun and Games

In the opening, double-page spread, the season is summer and the children and animals are engaged in a variety of outdoor games. Invite students to make a list of the games they are playing. Then ask them each to choose an individual favorite game from the list. Ask them to think about playing the game or engaging in the activity (such as kite flying). Consider what skills are required to do well in that game/activity. The strength may be a physical one, a strategic ability (as in hide-and-seek), or a mental ability such as a good imagination. Use the Fun and Games graphic organizer on page 16 to list the games and activities and the skills required. Invite each student to put his or her initials in the columns for the activities he or she most enjoys.

Then ask students to brainstorm a short list of other games that they enjoy which might have been pictured in the opening illustration. Again, ask them to consider what skills are required to do well in that game/activity. Complete the Fun and Games graphic organizer with these new games. Good resources for this activity include:

- *Acka Backa Boo! Playground Games from Around the World* by Opal Dunn with illustrations by Susan Winter. Henry Holt & Company, 2000.

- *Come Out and Play* by Maya Ajmera. Charlesbridge Publishing, 2002.

- *Games Kids Play*, www.gameskidsplay.net.

Life Skills Standards

Thinking and Reasoning

- Effectively uses mental processes that are based on identifying similarities and differences

Behavioral Studies Standards

- Understands that interactions among learning, inheritance, and physical development affect human behavior

Multiple Intelligences at Play

If you and your students have completed the Multiple Intelligences activity on page 123 for *Violet's Music*, continue your work on multiple intelligences by deciding, for each of the games/activities listed on the Fun and Games graphic organizer, which intelligence(s) the best player should possesses. Add that information to the graphic organizer in the row provided and reflect on the intelligences of members of the class to determine which activities would be best matched to each class member's strengths. Follow up by creating a large mural/bulletin board of the class engaging in these activities with the animals from *Book! Book! Book!*

Physical Education Standards

- Understands the social and personal responsibility associated with participation in physical activity

Life Skills Standards

Thinking and Reasoning

- Effectively uses mental processes that are based on identifying similarities and differences

Something to Do in the Library

When the farm animals in *Book! Book! Book!* get bored, they follow the hen into town to find something to do. Spotting people coming out of the public library, the animals decide to go in, one at a time. Ask students to study the illustrations that portray the inside of the public library and brainstorm a list of activities that one can do in that town's public library. Now invite students to add to this list by reflecting on their own experiences in public libraries in their town or others. What else might be added to the list?

A Trip to Town

As it turned out, the public library was the perfect place for the animals to go and find something wonderful to do. On another day and trip to town, however, they might also find other community places in their search for something to do. Invite students to list the many places in the community that the animals might go using the Trip to Town graphic organizer on page 17. Add the information about what they would find to do in each place.

Language Arts Connections

Animal Wordplay

One of the wonderful features of *Book! Book! Book!* is the wordplay involved with the animal's sounds. Begin by asking students to return to the text of the book and list the various animals with the sounds they make. Guide them in noting that both the hen and the frog make sounds that can be interpreted as words by humans in a particular situation. Then ask students to do some research in the library media center (using

the Internet or nonfiction and fiction books about farm animals) to come up with a list of other farm animals not included in Deborah Bruss's story. List the sound each one makes.

A useful resource for online information about farm animals is:

- *Farm Animals Around the World* www.enchantedlearning.com/ coloring/farm.shtml

A useful resource for online animal sounds is:

- *Sounds of the 4-H Farm* www.ics.uci.edu/~pazzani/4H/ Sounds.html

Language Arts Standards

Reading

- Uses the general skills and strategies of the reading process

- Uses reading skills and strategies to understand and interpret a variety of literary texts

- Uses reading skills and strategies to understand and interpret a variety of informational texts

Storytelling and Puppet Play

The final activity that the animals enjoy as a result of their trip to the public library is an evening book-sharing with puppets, modeled after the story hour in the library in which the librarian is using a puppet. Invite students to select one of the farm animal fiction books they found in the library media center during the Animal Wordplay activity (page 14) and present it to the class using one or more farm animal puppets. **Note:** If you do not have a collection of puppets in your school, you can make a set of paper bag or stick puppets using the coloring sheets at www.enchantedlearning. com/coloring/farm.shtml.

Language Arts Standards

Reading

- Uses the general skills and strategies of the reading process

Listening and Speaking

- Uses listening and speaking strategies for different purposes

Fun and Games

Game	Skills	Student Initials	Intelligences Needed
Tug-of-War			

Multiple Intelligences: Word Smart (Linguistic Intelligence); Number/Reasoning Smart (Logical/Mathematical Intelligence); Picture Smart (Spatial Intelligence); Body Smart (Bodily/Kinesthetic Intelligence); Music Smart (Musical Intelligence); People Smart (Interpersonal Intelligence); Self Smart (Intrapersonal Intelligence); Nature Smart (Naturalist Intelligence); Wondering Smart (Existential Intelligence).

Read! Perform! Learn! Book! Book! Book!

Trip to Town

On the inner circles, list other community locations where the animals might have gone to find something to do. On the outer circles, list activities the animals might find to do in each location.

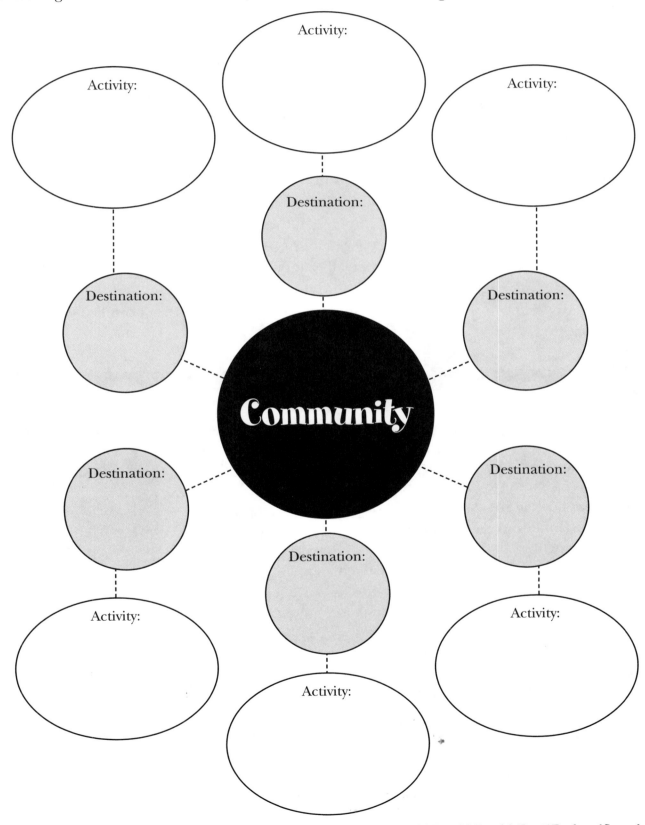

Activity:

Activity:

Activity:

Destination:

Destination:

Destination:

Community

Destination:

Destination:

Destination:

Activity:

Activity:

Activity:

Chicken Soup by Heart

Read *Chicken Soup by Heart* and the interview with Esther Hershenhorn below to familiarize yourself with the book and the author. Once you are ready to perform the script with your students, read the book aloud to the children so that they can enjoy the illustrations and become familiar with the story. Then, hand out a set of photocopied scripts to ten children. Ask the remaining children to be the audience. Have performers face the audience and simply read their parts on the first run-through. (Prepare students for some lively Yiddish expressions!) Once all readers are comfortable with their parts, have a second reading with the opportunity to use props or costumes, if desired, and to act out the story while reading.

Meet Esther Hershenhorn

Chicagoan Esther Hershenhorn spends her days doing what she loves and loving what she does—writing award-winning picture books and middle grade fiction, teaching adult Writing for Children classes, and coaching writers of all ages to help them tell their stories. Esther often visits classrooms across Illinois and the Midwest, facilitating Writing Workshops and celebrating young authors. Esther also serves as the Regional Advisor of the Illinois Chapter of the Society of Children's Book Writers and Illustrators, as well as on the international organization's Board of Directors, advocating children's books and their creators.

In *Chicken Soup by Heart*, **Mrs. Gittel is such a wonderful, nurturing character, the sort of person, whether a grandparent, an aunt or uncle, or an older friend, that every young person deserves to have in his or her life. What is your personal connection to Mrs. Gittel?**

EH: My son was lucky enough to have two grandmothers who not only adored him and couldn't do enough for him but who loved him unconditionally. They gladly indulged his every whim and passion, especially his passion for anything numerical. When he was a toddler, both grandmothers

would sit for hours at the window with him, counting cars and buses as they came and went. When he grew older, both spent even more hours playing all sorts of card games with him, praising his fine mind and allowing him to win, of course.

What were you like as a child? Were you like Rudie Dinkins, resourceful, generous, and a tiny bit crafty?

EH: I passed this question on to my dear, dear older sister, for the sake of objectivity. She responded that I always smiled and laughed, that I loved making other people smile and laugh, that I was lively and energetic and a lover of surprises.

One of the most delightful aspects of this story is the language, both the Yiddish words and expressions and the general cadence of the narrative. Will you talk a bit about this aspect of writing *Chicken Soup by Heart*?

EH: Which came first? The chicken soup or the Yiddish? I think I tossed in all sorts of ingredients, if you will, while cooking up this story, including those two grandmothers again, one of whom made the World's Best Chicken Soup and called my son her *zeesah* boy, her sweet, sweet boy, and the other who often peppered her conversations with Russian and Yiddish and labeled my son her *boychik*. I also added All Things Jewish, including holidays and Klezmer music.

The structure of *Chicken Soup by Heart* is also very interesting. You've used the rule of three as well as a double-layered frame story structure. Will you talk about how this complex and satisfying structure evolved?

EH: When writing a story, I always look for that one song that sounds like my story, that captures its heart, that expresses its essence. I listened to literally hundreds of Klezmer songs until the Klezmer Conservatory Band served up the winner—their version of the well-known children's riddle song "Tum Balalayka." The back-and-forth questioning within the song approximated the reciprocity of Rudie's and Mrs. Gittel's friendship. "What can cry and shed no tears?" the riddler asks. "A harts," came the reply. "A harts." *Harts* is Yiddish for heart. I recognized my story in this song instantly. I knew, too, instinctively that there would be more to my story than just a straightforward telling. I would tell a story within a story to underscore their love.

How can readers learn more about you and your books?

EH: They can visit my Web site at www. estherhershenhorn.com.

Books by Esther Hershenhorn

Chicken Soup by Heart illustrated by Rosanne Litzinger. Simon & Schuster, 2002.

Confe$$ion$ and $ecret$ of Howard J. Fingerhut illustrated by Ethan Long. Holiday House, 2002.

Fancy That illustrated by Megan Lloyd. Holiday House, 2003.

I Is for Illinois illustrated by Rebecca Havekost. GHB Publishers, 2001.

Illinois Fun Facts and Games illustrated by Eileen Balcom-Vetillo. GHB Publishers, 2001.

There Goes Lowell's Party illustrated by Jacqueline Rogers. Holiday House, 1998.

Chicken Soup by Heart Script

Roles

Mama

Mrs. Gittel

Rudie Dinkins

Narrator One

Narrator Two

Narrator Three

Chorus (Four readers)

Chorus:	Here it is from start to finish: how such a nice *boychik* saved the Chicken Soup Queen.
Narrator One:	It was a very nice Sunday in the middle of spring, in the middle of breakfast, in the middle of the morning. Rudie Dinkins heard his Mama say ...
Mama:	Rudie, your sitter Mrs. Gittel has the flu.
Narrator Two:	Rudie ran down the hallway to Mrs. Gittel's apartment.
Chorus:	Before he ever *k-nocked,* he heard
Mrs. Gittel:	A-choo! A-choo! A-choo! A-choo! A-choo! A-choo! A-choo! A-choo! A-choo! A-choo! A-choo! A-choo! A-choo!
Rudie Dinkins:	*(Shout.)* It's me! My mama says you're sick!
Narrator Three:	Mrs. Gittel sneezed again, then blew her nose twice. She whispered through the door.
Mrs. Gittel:	*(Whisper.) Oy!* You can't come in, Rudie.
Narrator One:	Rudie Dinkins had some Very Big Worries now. So big, in fact, he had to sit down to think about them.
Rudie Dinkins:	What if it was me who made Mrs. Gittel sick?
Narrator Two:	Only last week he'd had a Rudie Dinkins Chest Cold.
Rudie Dinkins:	Who will snug-a-bug her like she snug-a-bugged me? Who will cook her chicken soup and make her good as new?
Narrator Three:	There was also some supposing as to when she'd be all better. Mrs. Gittel baby-sat him Mondays after school.
Chorus:	Rudie *k-nocked* again.

Rudie Dinkins: (*Shout.*) Don't worry! I'm cooking you chicken soup. You'll be good as new tonight.

Narrator One: In a minute Rudie stood in the middle of his kitchen. This was no small task, cooking Mrs. Gittel chicken soup.

Narrator Two: Mrs. Gittel was the Chicken Soup Queen. She deserved the very best, namely, soup the way *she* cooked it.

Chorus: Lucky thing!

Narrator Three: After all his chest colds, Rudie knew her recipe, give or take an ingredient.

Chorus: Another lucky thing!

Narrator Three: He knew Mrs. Gittel's Chicken Soup secret! She stirred in very nice stories about her soon-to-be soup-eaters.

Narrator One: Rudie grabbed his mama and his mama grabbed a soup pot. Together they filled it so-high with water.

Narrator Two: Into the pot went some chicken and a chicken wing, plus a very nice wishbone Rudie'd saved for Mrs. Gittel.

Mama: I'll just stay nearby, in case my *boychik* spills.

Narrator Three: Of course, leave it to him to sneak in a Rudie Dinkins Surprise! Guess who knew his sitter liked her soup a little sweet?

Chorus: This is the first Mrs. Gittel story Rudie stirred in.

Narrator One: It was all about the time maybe three months back when he happened to have a Rudie Dinkins Chest Cold.

Narrator Two: Mrs. Gittel baby-sat him and like always, made him chicken soup.

Narrator Three: It was Number Day at school, though. He was very sad to miss it. So while the soup cooked they practiced counting like accountants!

Narrator One: They counted soup spoons and soup nuts and cousins in the picture frames, then love-seat flowers and cowboys on his quilt.

Narrator Two: Next chin hairs and liver spots and beauty marks and freckles.

Narrator Three:	Every ten numbers they would share a candy Kiss. When they were done they'd counted almost to a thousand!
Mrs. Gittel:	You're a regular genius!
Narrator One:	Which was certainly the truth.
Narrator Two:	Only such a smart *boychik* could shoo Mrs. Gittel's flu bug.
Narrator Three:	Rudie brought his chest-cold cream to Mrs. Gittel's door.
Rudie Dinkins:	*(Shout.)* It's me!
Chorus:	He *k-nocked* again.
Rudie Dinkins:	*(Shout.)* How are you?
Mrs. Gittel:	*Oy-oy-oy!* Don't ask, Rudie.
Narrator One:	So in less than a minute Rudie was back in the middle of his kitchen cooking Mrs. Gittel chicken soup.
Mama:	I'll chop some nice vegetable chunks.
Narrator Two:	Rudie added the carrots and a little bit of celery.
Narrator Three:	And leave it to him to sneak in *another* Rudie Surprise! Guess who knew his sitter liked her soup a little sweet?
Chorus:	This is the second Mrs. Gittel story Rudie stirred in.
Narrator One:	It was all about the time he stopped by Mrs. Gittel's apartment to give her a look at his brand-new wagon.
Narrator Two:	It was Mrs. Gittel's card game day. Her fingers ached like crazy.
Narrator Three:	Mrs. Gittel asked him could he stay and give a help.
Narrator One:	So Rudie helped shuffle and Rudie helped deal and Rudie picked a card whenever Mrs. Gittel's turn came.
Narrator Two:	The two of them would whisper, rearranging their cards.
Narrator Three:	Rudie's job was shouting ...
Rudie Dinkins:	Gin! We win!
Narrator Three:	Every jelly bean in the candy dish was Rudie's.
Mrs. Gittel:	They should bottle you like medicine!
Narrator One:	Which was also the truth.
Narrator Two:	Only such a helpful boy would know which pocket had his cough drops.

Read! Perform! Learn! Chicken Soup by Heart

Narrator Three:	Rudie wrapped up two to bring to Mrs. Gittel's door.
Rudie Dinkins:	*(Shout.)* It's me!
Chorus:	He *k-nocked* again.
Rudie Dinkins:	*(Shout.)* How are you?
Mrs. Gittel:	*Ei-Ei-Ei!* I'm too sick to *Oy!*
Narrator One:	It took twenty seconds tops for Rudie to get back to the middle of his kitchen to finish making chicken soup.
Mama:	I'll peel an onion and chop it into nice chunks.
Narrator Two:	Rudie held his nose and added the onion.
Narrator Three:	Leave it to him to sneak in one last Surprise! Guess who knew his sitter liked her soup a little sweet?
Chorus:	This is the last Mrs. Gittel story Rudie stirred in.
Narrator One:	It was all about the time when Rudie's Mama worked a Saturday and Mrs. Gittel's Arthur moved too far away to visit.
Narrator Two:	Rudie and Mrs. Gittel couldn't make a smile no-how, so they walked up the avenue to have themselves a good time.
Narrator Three:	They watched a parade and posed for pictures in a picture booth.
Mrs. Gittel:	You're movie-star handsome!
Narrator One:	Then they stopped and had a bite and *schmoozed* with Mrs. Gittel's girlfriends.
Rudie Dinkins:	You should have your own talk show!
Narrator Two:	Later they were so pooped that they had to rest their tootsies. Mrs.Gittel hugged him.
Mrs. Gittel:	We're some very good friends.
Chorus:	Truer words a person never spoke.
Narrator Three:	Right then Rudie grabbed those pictures, Mama loaded up his wagon, and he wheeled his chicken soup to Mrs. Gittel's door.
Rudie Dinkins:	*(Shout.)* It's me!
Chorus:	He *k-nocked, k-nocked, k-nocked.*

Rudie Dinkins: I made you chicken soup with three Mrs. Gittel stories! Mama said you should cook it up hot. How are you anyway?

Mrs. Gittel: You don't want to know!

Narrator One: Well, what a person wouldn't want to know is how Rudie slept that night. He had such crazy nightmares in the middle of his head.

Narrator Two: All a person needs to know is how Rudie woke up, with a hurt in his middle and a *k-nock* at the door.

Narrator Three: Rudie gave a listen.

Mrs. Gittel: Where's our favorite *boychik*?

Narrator Three: Rudie gave a peek.

Rudie Dinkins: *(Shout.)* Mrs. Gittel! My chicken soup worked!

Mrs. Gittel: You knew my recipe by heart! Plus, leave it to you to make it Rudie Dinkins sweet!

Rudie Dinkins: *(Moan.) Ooooo! Ooooo! Ooooo! Ooooo!*

Mrs. Gittel: *Oy!* That's a Rudie Dinkins Tummy-ache!

Narrator One: So Mrs. Gittel baby-sat him and snug-a-bugged him tight and in the middle of the morning fixed him a seltzer.

Narrator Two: They played a little cards and they talked and looked at pictures.

Narrator Three: Then they made chicken soup to have for supper later.

Chorus: The two of them together stirred in such a nice story.

Mrs. Gittel: Here it is, from start to finish: how such a nice *boychik* saved the Chicken Soup Queen ...

The End

Chicken Soup by Heart Activities

Language Arts Connections

A Story within a Story

Discuss the structure of *Chicken Soup by Heart* with students. Not only does the book contain three internal stories—the story about Number Day, the story about playing cards, and the story about the trip around town, but the book itself is one extended story about the day that Mrs. Gittel got sick and Rudie made her chicken soup.

Ask students to diagram the story as a set of internal stories within a frame story in order to better understand the way the plot is unfolding. **Note:** If you use Kidspiration® software in your school, your students can complete this assignment electronically.

Next, consider undertaking a writing project in which you follow Esther Hershenhorn's lead. Create a story about your class as a whole that serves as a frame story to a collection of individual stories told by each student. Essential to the success of this project is an over-arching theme to the story. Friendship and mutual love and support are the themes of *Chicken Soup by Heart* and may be the perfect themes for your story, too!

More Stories within Stories

The story-within-a-story format is a timeless structure and an interesting one to examine in children's literature. With your students, gather a collection of books that utilize this format. Discuss how this structure works and the meaning of the term "frame story." Then, study the way the author uses the frame and internal stories. As you share each book with students, ask them these questions:

- What is the frame story about?

- What is the internal story, the "story within a story," about? (Note that there may be more than one.)

- What do you think the author's theme/ message is?

- How does the "story within a story" structure help the author?

- How do the two (or more) stories work together to deepen the theme/get the author's message across?

You will find an excellent annotated bibliography prepared by Library Media Specialist and Education Professor Judi Moreillon, Ph.D., online at storytrail.com/ pdf/MoreillonStoriesinStoriesbib.pdf.

Dressing Up a Story

Author Esther Hershenhorn dresses up *Chicken Soup by Heart* with many Yiddish words and phrases, beginning on the first page when she writes:

"Here it is from start to finish: how such a nice *boychik* saved the Chicken Soup Queen."

Ask students to identify each of the Yiddish words or phrases they encounter in the book and list them on the Dressing up a Story graphic organizer on page 28. The author did not include a glossary in the book because she trusted that each of these words would either be familiar to American readers or that young readers would be able to determine their meaning from the context in which they were used. Invite your students to speculate, as informed readers, about the meaning of each of the Yiddish words or phrases and, once they are in agreement, list their definitions next to each word. Finally, use the online Yiddish glossary at www.pass.to/glossary/Default.htm to discover the actual definition of each word or phrase and record it on the graphic organizer as well. **Note:** Be aware that you may not want to send students to this glossary on their own as it also contains Yiddish expletives.

Music Connection

Klezmer Music

In her interview, Esther Hershenhorn says that for each book she writes, she looks for a single song that "sounds like" her story and then uses that song to inform her writing. For *Chicken Soup by Heart* it was the Klezmer lullaby "Tum Balalayka." You can listen to an online sound clip of this song recorded by Theodore Bikel at www.bikel.com/sound_clips.html. To read the lyrics of the song in both English and Yiddish, visit www.rhymesandsongs.com/nursery_rhymes/greensleeves.html and click on the Tum Balalayka link.

After reading the lyrics, ask students to discuss the author's statement that "The back-and-forth questioning within the song approximated the reciprocity of Rudie's and Mrs. Gittel's friendship."

You might also want to introduce your students to the broader field of Klezmer music at the Zemerl interactive database of Jewish songs online at www.zemerl.com. Type "Klezmer" into the search box to locate a list of Klezmer songs. As you click each song title, you will find a page that includes a link to an online sound file.

Social Studies Connection

Friendship Across Generations

The centerpiece of *Chicken Soup by Heart* is the friendship between Rudie Dinkins and Mrs. Gittel. A special, intergenerational relationship, whether with a grandparent, sitter, family friend, or uncle or aunt, is one of the most treasured relationships in a child's life. Encourage students to talk about the special supportive relationships they share with adults other than their parents as you begin this activity.

First, as a group complete the Friendship across Generations graphic organizer on page 29 for Rudie Dinkins, with Rudie and Mrs. Gittel at the center. List three things that Rudie and Mrs. Gittel like to do together in the inner ring of circles. Then ask students what important "gift" each of the friends gets from the activity. For instance, how does it make Mrs. Gittel feel when Rudie helps her with the card playing? How does it make Rudie feel?

Next, ask students to complete the graphic organizer with themselves and their own intergenerational friend at the center.

Behavioral Studies Standards

- Understands that group and cultural influences contribute to human development, identity, and behavior

- Understands various meanings of social group, general implications of group membership, and different ways that groups function

Life Skills Standards

Working with Others

- Works well with diverse individuals and in diverse situations

Mathematics Connections

Number Day

When Rudie had a Rudie Dinkins Chest Cold, he had to miss Number Day at school, which made him sad. But Mrs. Gittel and Rudie spent the day practicing counting in the apartment like accountants and then ate a candy Kiss for each ten things they counted. Challenge students to brainstorm a list of things in the library, classroom, or school that could be counted and decide on a healthy reward they might eat for every ten they count. Then ask each student to count one of the collections and record the number counted and the number of treats per student on a chart.

Mathematics Standards

- Understands and applies basic and advanced properties of the concepts of numbers

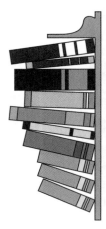

Dressing Up a Story

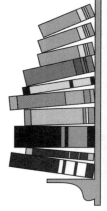

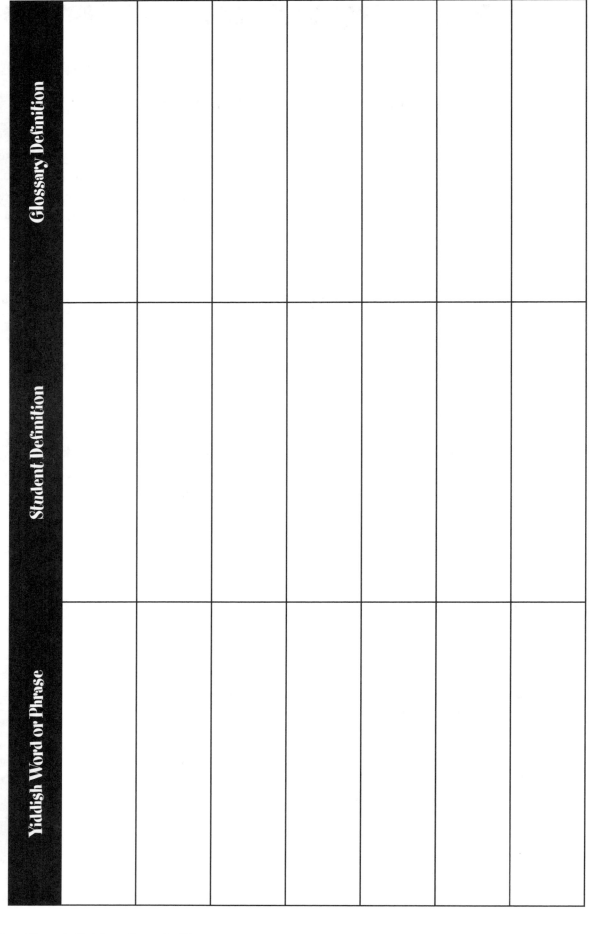

Yiddish Word or Phrase	Student Definition	Glossary Definition

Read! Perform! Learn! Chicken Soup by Heart

Friendship Across Generations

In the center circle, write your name and your older friend's name. In the "we like to" circles, write something you like to do with your friend. In the "gift" circles, list the gift each friend receives from the activity.

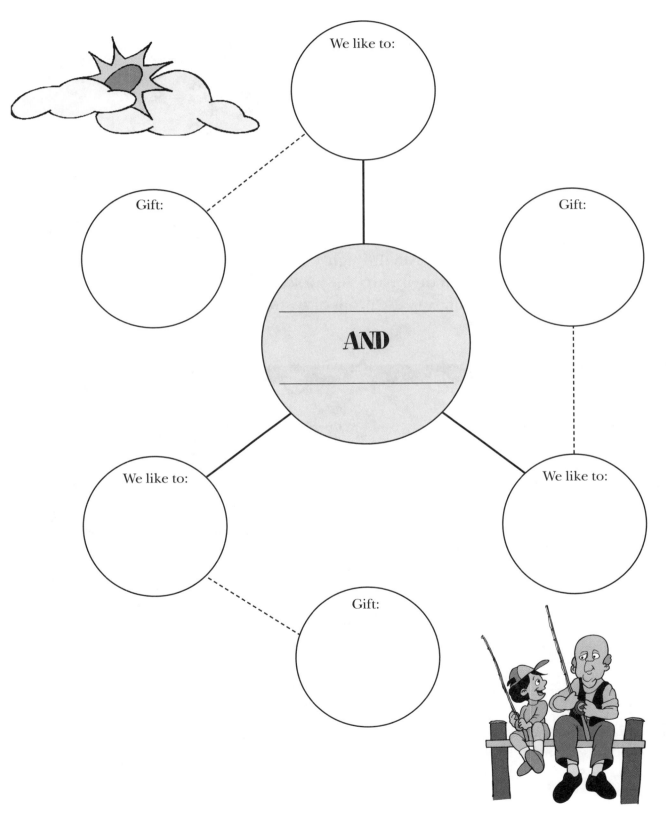

Dinosnores

Read *Dinosnores* and the interview with Kelly DiPucchio below to familiarize yourself with the book and the author. Once you are ready to perform the script with your students, read the book aloud to the children so that they can enjoy the illustrations and become familiar with the story. If you wish to have your students do a pre-reading activity, see Snore Fest on page 36. Then, hand out a set of photocopied scripts to 15 children. Ask the remaining children to be the audience. Have performers face the audience and simply read their parts on the first run-through. Once all readers are comfortable with their parts, have a second reading with the opportunity to use props or costumes, if desired, and to act out the story while reading.

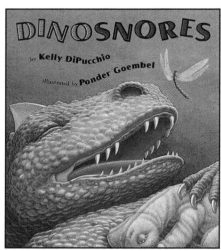

Meet Kelly DiPucchio

Kelly DiPucchio was born during the Cenozoic era, "sometime after the age of dinosaurs and before the invention of the cordless phone." As a child, Kelly loved dinosaurs and sleeping so it came as no surprise to her family and teachers that she grew up to write a book called *Dinosnores*. Kelly attended college at Michigan State University where her favorite subjects included anthropology, creative writing, and coffee. She is also the author of *Bed Hogs, Liberty's Journey,* and *What's the Magic Word?* Kelly rewrites history from her home in Michigan, where she lives with her husband and three dino-mite kids.

Dinosnores is a story about one of the most popular subjects of elementary school children. But you're an adult! How did you come to write a dinosaur book?

KD: Some people might argue whether or not I'm an adult, but we'll save that discussion for another time. Actually, *Dinosnores* started with just a title. One night, my oldest daughter said, "Daddy has loud dino-snores!" I immediately thought that "Dinosnores" sounded like a great title for a book. After some quick research, I was very surprised to discover that nobody had ever written a book

using that title before. And no, I do not give my daughter a percentage of my royalties for giving me the idea. She gets paid in chicken nuggets and designer jeans.

There are many fabulous prehistoric details in your lively text. How much research did you have to do to write this story?

KD: I did do a fair amount of research for this particular picture book, which included playing with little plastic dinosaurs on the floor with my son. When I begin any new fictional story, I often go to the library and create extensive word lists from nonfiction books. I've found that these diversified word lists give my creative writing a wonderful jumpstart.

Like your picture books *Bed Hogs, Liberty's Journey,* and *What's the Magic Word?, Dinosnores* is written in rhymed verse. Why have you chosen to write in rhyme, and what challenges do you face as you do? Do you have forthcoming books written in prose?

KD: In most cases, I don't "choose" to write a story in rhyme. The rhyme chooses me. When I get a new story idea, I often wait to "hear" the first lines, or snippets of the story in my head. When those lines come to me in rhyme, I usually groan because writing in rhyme can be a real challenge at times. I think the hardest thing about writing in rhyme is revising in rhyme! But when a rhyming story clicks, and everything finally comes together, it can be very exhilarating, kind of like finishing a *New York Times* crossword puzzle.

I do have two forthcoming picture books that were written in prose—*Mrs. McBloom,*

Clean Up Your Classroom! and *Grace For President.* I have to say, I really enjoy prose, and I'm much less likely to chew off my fingernails, throw tantrums, and sprout gray hairs during the writing process.

The language in *Dinosnores* is a great deal of fun; you seem to specialize in puns, wordplay, and alliterative pairings here. Was this a particular pleasure for you in writing this book?

KD: Oooh, I like that! I might use that as an advertising slogan on my business card: "Specializing in Puns, Wordplay, and Alliterative Pairings." It is true that I really love to write and read picture books with multi-layered humor. I think the most successful picture books are those that appeal to both children and adults. When I'm reading picture books to my children, I always appreciate any sophisticated, hidden humor, whether it's in the text or in the illustrations.

***Dinosnores* is a part of the long literary tradition of "pourquoi tales." Did you purposely set out to write a pourquoi tale (stories designed to explain a natural phenomenon or the existence of something in nature) or was it serendipity?**

KD: *Non! C'était une coincidence!* Hey, my four years of high school French is finally paying off! Seriously, I did not set out to write a "pourquoi tale." In fact, I'd never heard that term before! As I mentioned, *Dinosnores* started with just a title that I had to build a story around. I thought about dinosaurs and what repercussions might have come about from their loud snoring. That line of thinking led me on a very

tumultuous trip back in time that included earthquakes, mudslides, and volcanic eruptions. Once I had my convoluted geological theory in place, the story took off and essentially wrote itself.

How can readers learn more about you and your books?

KD: Well, they could knock on my door and ask me, but I don't recommend that because they're likely to catch me with bedhead and coffee breath. Or they could bribe me for information by sending me ridiculously flattering fan mail and expensive chocolates. (I highly recommend this option.) But probably the easiest way to learn more about me and my books is to visit my Web site at www.kellydipucchio. com.

Books by Kelly DiPucchio

Bed Hogs illustrated by Howard Fine. Hyperion, 2004.

Dinosnores illustrated by Ponder Goembel. HarperCollins, 2005.

Grace for President. Hyperion, 2008.

Liberty's Journey illustrated by Richard Egielski. Hyperion, 2004.

Monster Makeovers illustrated by LeUyen Pham. Hyperion, 2006.

Mrs. McBloom, Clean Up Your Classroom! illustrated by Guy Francis. Hyperion, 2005.

Sipping Spiders through a Straw illustrated by Gris Grimly. Scholastic, Forthcoming.

What's the Magic Word? illustrated by Marsha Winborn. HarperCollins, 2005.

Dinosnores Script

> **Roles**
>
> | | | | |
> |---|---|---|---|
> | Brontosaurus | Stegosaurus | Allosaurus | Narrator Two |
> | Triceratops | Protoceratops | Tyrannosaurus | Narrator Three |
> | Raptor | Diplodocus | Narrator One | Narrator Four |
> | Chorus (Three readers) | | | |

Narrator One:	On a super continent many million years ago,
Narrator Two:	dinosaurs prepared for sleep on cozy lava flows.
Chorus:	YAWN!
Narrator Three:	They bathed, and brushed, and fluffed their ferns around the dino site …
Narrator Four:	then laid their horns and spikes to rest and kissed their eggs good night.
Chorus:	SMOOOCH!
Narrator One:	Reptilian birds and dragonflies drifted through the skies,
Narrator Two:	while prehistoric crickets sang Jurassic lullabies.
Chorus:	CHIRRUP!
Narrator Three:	Soon the peaceful world was rocked, shaken to its shores …
Narrator Four:	from snouts of sleeping dinosaurs boomed mammoth dino-snores!
Chorus:	ZZZZZZZZZZZZZZ!
Narrator One:	There were …
Brontosaurus:	Bronto-booms,
Triceratops:	Tricera-cries,
Raptor:	Raptor-rumbles,
Stegosaurus:	Stego-sighs …
Protoceratops:	Proto-grunts,

Diplodocus:	Diplo-hoots,
Allosaurus:	Allo-snorts,
Tyrannosaurus:	Tyranno-toots!
Narrator One:	While dinos slept, winged lizards leapt and mammals ran to hide.
Narrator Two:	Palm trees quivered. Hot springs shivered. Bugs were petrified!
Chorus:	ZZZZZZZZZZZZZ!
Narrator Three:	Still sleepy rumbling kept on coming from that dino chorus.
Narrator Four:	Whistles, grunts, and snorts galore sprang from every 'saurus!
All Dinosaurs:	WHISTLE! GRUNT! SNORT!
Narrator One:	Their nasal breeze stirred up the seas and wind storms full of sand.
Narrator Two:	Swamps and rivers sloshed about—tossed creatures onto land.
Chorus:	BOOM! CRY! RUMBLE! SIGH … GRUNT! HOOT! SNORT! TOOT!
Narrator Three:	That rumpus triggered tremors and a powerful earthquake.
Narrator Four:	The shaking scared amphibians and drove them from the lake.
Chorus:	CRASH! SPLASH!
Narrator One:	Dino drools made swimming pools and gooey, slick mudslides.
Narrator Two:	Sharks and ancient giant squids surfed slimy spit riptides.
Chorus:	DUDE! WIPEOUT!
Narrator Three:	Deep grumbles made rocks tumble and loud Cretaceous booms!
Narrator Four:	Chains of sleeping mountain tops awoke in fiery plumes.
Chorus:	KA-BOOM!

Narrator One:	After several million nights like this of snoring from the pit,
Narrator Two:	the shaken supercontinent began to crack and split!
Chorus:	CRRRRRRACK!
Narrator Three:	The dinos waved good-bye to friends and drifted off to sea.
Narrator Four:	As for the rest, you may have guessed …
All Dinosaurs:	It's ancient history.

The End

Dinosnores Activities

Language Arts Connections

Snore Fest

Author Kelly DiPucchio chose eight dinosaurs to include in *Dinosnores*. Before reading the reader's theater (which names the individual dinosaurs), supply small groups of students with a variety of dinosaur resources and the Snore Fest graphic organizer from page 39. Ask them to identify the name of each dinosaur—using the dinosnores as clues!

Good resources for this activity include:

Print

The Dinosaur Atlas by Don Lessem. Firefly Books, 2003.

Dinosaur Dictionary: An A to Z of Dinosaurs and Prehistoric Reptiles by Rupert Matthews. Blackbirch Press, 2003.

Encyclopedia Prehistorica: Dinosaurs by Robert Sabuda and Matthew Reinhart. Candlewick Press, 2005.

Scholastic Dinosaurs A-Z: The Ultimate Dinosaur Encyclopedia by Don Lessem. Scholastic, 2003.

Electronic

A to Z Glossary
yahooligans.yahoo.com/content/science/dinosaurs/glossary/glossarya.html

Dinosaur Alphabet Book
www.enchantedlearning.com/dinoalphabet

Language Arts Standards

Writing

* Gathers and uses information for research purposes

Reading

* Uses reading skills and strategies to understand and interpret a variety of informational texts

Snore Some More

Begin by brainstorming snoring sounds other than the eight that Kelly DiPucchio used in her story. List them on the board or a chart that all students can see. Invite student groups to continue their research and choose eight additional dinosaurs, creating a snore for each one by combining the start of its name, a hyphen, and a sound word to accompany it.

Language Arts Standards

Writing

* Gathers and uses information for research purposes

Porquoi?

Explain pourquoi tales (stories designed to explain a natural phenomenon or the existence of something in nature) to students and read some other examples, including:

Arrow to the Sun: A Pueblo Indian Tale by Gerald McDermott. Viking, 1974.

A Collection of Rudyard Kipling's Just So Stories by Rudyard Kipling, illustrated by Cathie Felstead and Christopher Corr. Candlewick Press, 2004.

Rainbow Crow: A Lenape Tale by Nancy Van Laan, illustrated by Beatriz Vidal. Knopf, 1989.

Why Mosquitoes Buzz in People's Ears: A West African Tale by Verna Aardema, illustrated by Leo Dillon. Dial, 1998.

Invite students to discuss *Dinosnores* as a pourquoi tale. How does it fit the definition? Then lead the class in creating a new pourquoi tale. Begin by brainstorming to identify something in nature they would like to explain in a creative way. Once the natural element or phenomenon is chosen, brainstorm to create a list of possible origins (aim for creativity and logic). Then, as a group, write the new pourquoi tale (act as the scribe for the group and write the story on chart paper).

For more help in teaching the writing of pourquoi tales, you can find a PowerPoint presentation online at Writing a Pourquoi Story, k12.albemarle.org/MurrayElem/ Estep/Library/Projects_Estep/Writing%2 0a%20Pourquoi%20PowerPt.html.

If desired, supply students with copies of the final story printed in book format and ask each child—or small groups—to illustrate it.

Language Arts Standards

Reading

- Uses reading skills and strategies to understand and interpret a variety of literary texts

Writing

- Uses the stylistic and rhetorical aspects of writing

Dino Voice

Invite each student to select one dinosaur from Kelly DiPucchio's dinos in *Dinosnores*. Ask students to think about the dinosaur they have chosen. They might even be invited to return to the resources suggested in Snore Fest (page 36). What kind of creature is their dino? Is it friendly, cranky, sad, cheerful, fierce, peaceful, etc.? Once students have defined their dinosaur using two or three adjectives, ask them to retell the story from the point of view of their chosen dinosaur, with an emphasis on voice. The adjectives they have chosen will help them to do so.

Language Arts Standards

Writing

- Uses the stylistic and rhetorical aspects of writing

- Gathers and uses information for research purposes

Listening and Speaking

- Uses listening and speaking strategies for different purposes

Science Connections

Supercontinent!

Share a map of the earth with its seven continents labeled (or provide an individual black line continent map to each student, available at fga.freac.fsu.edu/pdf/world/ world_blank.pdf) and help them to label the continents. Discuss the location of their state and country on the map and identify the other six continents as well.

Introduce the idea of the supercontinent of Pangaea. You might want to project the interactive NASA game at <u>kids.mtpe.hq.nasa.gov/archive/pangaea/Pangaea_game.html</u> allowing students to identify today's continents on the former supercontinent. Now share the series of continent maps, beginning with Pangaea, available at <u>geology.com/pangea.htm</u> and discuss scientific theories of the break-up of the continents.

Ask students how Kelly DiPucchio brought real science into her book *Dinosnores* to create a fanciful explanation for the creation of the seven continents as they exist today.

> ### Science Standards
>
> **Earth and Space Sciences**
>
> - Understands Earth's composition and structure

Time for Dinos

What was the earth like during the time of the dinosaurs? Invite students to research the Triassic, Jurassic, and Cretaceous eras of the earth's history, recording facts about each on the Time for Dinos graphic organizer on page 40. You may have books in your library media center that will serve as good resources. A good online resource for this activity is Dinopedia, <u>yahooligans.yahoo.com/content/science/dinosaurs/glossary/glossarya.html</u>. Click on each era on the left sidebar, then scroll down to the bottom toolbar and click on **More** under Ecology.

Invite students to create a prehistoric time line, recording their research findings for each era on the time line and drawing scenes based on the images they may have seen in their research.

> ### Science Standards
>
> **Life Sciences**
>
> - Understands relationships among organisms and their physical environment

Dino Eras

Using the eight dinosaurs identified in Snore Fest (page 36) and the additional dinosaurs identified in Snore Some More (page 36), ask students to research the era of each dinosaur. Now invite students to draw each dinosaur, cut the dinosaurs out, and place each one on the time line in the appropriate era.

> ### Science Standards
>
> **Life Sciences**
>
> - Understands relationships among organisms and their physical environment
>
> - Understands biological evolution and the diversity of life

Snore Fest

Dinosaur	Dinosnore	Dinosaur	Dinosnore
	Bronto-booms		
	Tricera-cries		
	Raptor-rumbles		
	Stego-sighs		
	Proto-grunts		
	Diplo-hoots		
	Allo-snorts		
	Tyranno-toots		

Time for Dinos

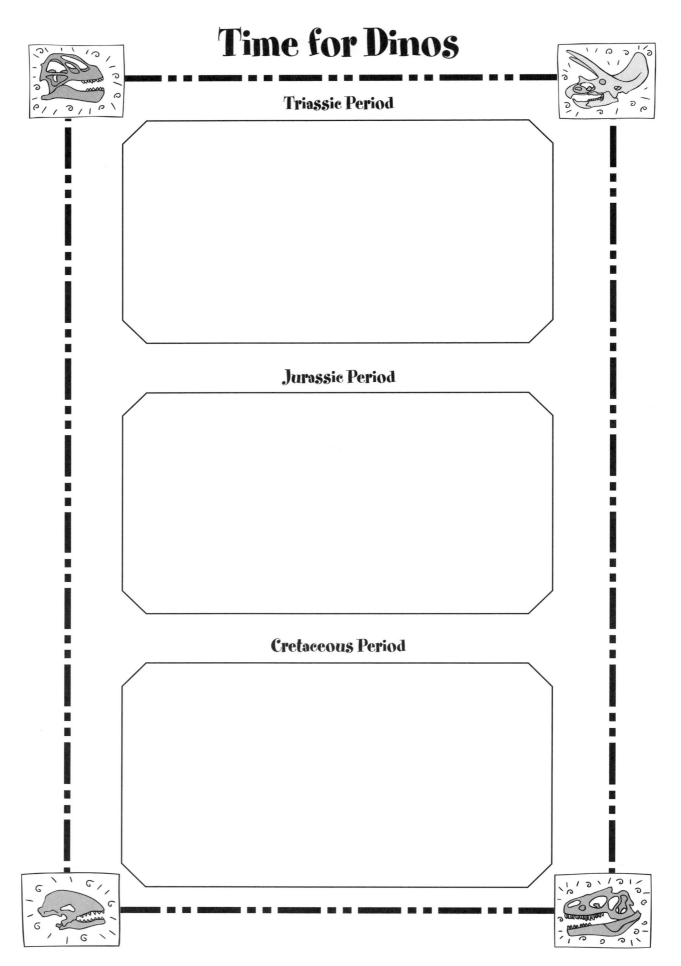

Triassic Period

Jurassic Period

Cretaceous Period

Jingle Dancer

Read *Jingle Dancer* and the interview with Cynthia Leitich Smith below to familiarize yourself with the book and the author. Once you are ready to perform the script with your students, read the book aloud to the children so that they can enjoy the illustrations and become familiar with the story. Then, hand out a set of photocopied scripts to 12 children. Ask the remaining children to be the audience. Have performers face the audience and simply read their parts on the first run-through. Once all readers are comfortable with their parts, have a second reading with the opportunity to act out the story while reading.

Meet Cynthia Leitich Smith

Cynthia Leitich Smith is the multi-award-winning author of *Jingle Dancer, Rain Is Not My Indian Name,* and *Indian Shoes.* She has also published middle grade and young adult short stories. Her next release will be a YA Gothic fantasy novel published by Candlewick Press in fall 2006. Smith was named a Writer of the Year in Children's Prose by Wordcraft Circle of Native Writers and Storytellers and spoke as a featured author at the Second National Book Festival. Her Web site at <u>www.cynthialeitich</u> <u>smith.com</u> was named one of the top ten writer sites on the Internet by *Writer's Digest,* and it was recognized among "Great Sites for Kids" by the American Library Association. She also maintains a blog at <u>cynthialeitichsmith.blogspot.com</u>; lives in

Austin, Texas; and is married to author Greg Leitich Smith.

Does *Jingle Dancer* arise from your own life experiences? If so, how?

CLS: Yes and no. Like Jenna, I'm a Muscogee (Creek) tribal member, who has lived in Oklahoma and has strong ties to women of each generation of her family and intertribal community. In addition, Jenna's cousin Elizabeth's legal career was inspired by my own educational and professional background in law. I also named a few of the characters—Mrs. Scott, Great-aunt Sis, and Cousin Elizabeth—after family members and asked that the illustrators,

Cornelius Van Wright and Ying-Hwa Hu, reflect our tribe's interracial population in their illustrations. However, I'm not coordinated enough to be a powwow dancer, although I did take tap and jazz for several years.

Jingle Dancer is a story that focuses on community in a way very personal to your main character. Can you talk about the role of community in Jenna's life and your own?

CLS: To Jenna, her tribal town and more broadly, the intertribal population of Oklahoma, are sort of sub-communities within the wider world. She both draws strength and lessons from them and also makes what contributions she can.

Like anyone, I have my immediate family, neighborhood, the city and state in which I live and those where I've lived in the past. I'm also a member of my tribe and of the children's YA literature community. For the latter, I make every effort to raise awareness of the need for contemporary Native books for young readers and the importance of quality literature, of trade books as a whole.

A key facet of the community in Jingle Dancer is that it is multi-generational. How does this reflect your own life?

CLS: My great-grandparents, grandparents, great aunts, great uncles, and other elders have always been active participants in my life and perspective. From my childhood, I clearly remember fishing on a pontoon boat in Oklahoma with my great-grandpa Ernest, visiting Grandma Melba who sold ladies dresses at the local JCPenney, taking turns with my cousin Stacy to try to "steal" a spot on my Grampa Clifford's chair, and lis-

tening to my Grandma Dorothy tell stories about her own mother, who died too young and was quite beautiful.

In my writing, I return again and again to the theme of intergenerational relationships as with Aunt Georgia in *Rain Is Not My Indian Name,* Grampa Halfmoon in *Indian Shoes,* and my recent short story "The Naked Truth" from *In My Grandmother's House: Award-Winning Authors Tell Stories About Their Grandmothers,* edited and illustrated by Bonnie Christensen.

Please talk about the aspect of reciprocity in the story. In what way is this reciprocity an essential attribute of Jenna's community?

CLS: Essentially, Jenna gives back to those who give to her. She is not simply "a taker," but rather someone who appreciates others' time and efforts and tries to offer the best she has to give in return. For example, Great-aunt Sis tells her a traditional story, and Jenna dances at the powwow in her honor and that of the other important women in her life.

Jingle Dancer is a very carefully structured story. Jenna moves through her community in a deliberate fashion, east, south, west, then north, as Sun moves in a half-circle across the sky. Please tell us more about the structure of your story and its importance.

CLS: Essentially, the story has a balance to it and a circular structure. Many cultures use a circular structure in storytelling, but most European and American traditions draw on the number three—three pigs, three Billy goats, the Trinity.

But Native cultures tend to draw more on the balance of the natural world—four directions, four stages of life, four colors of man, and, here, four rows of jingles.

Historically, American children's literature has offered us stories of Native people told not only from a non-Indian point of view but also in stylistically non-Indian ways. What I've tried to do with some of my Native writing is to draw more on our own storytelling and literary traditions in an effort to more fully expose all young readers to our worldview.

How can readers learn more about you and your books?

CLS: I manage an extensive children's literature Web site with biographical information and listings of recent interviews at www.cynthialeitichsmith.com.

Books by Cynthia Leitich Smith

Indian Shoes illustrated by Jim Madsen. HarperCollins, 2002.

In My Grandmother's House: Award-Winning Authors Tell Stories About Their Grandmothers edited and illustrated by Bonnie Christensen. HarperCollins, 2003.

Jingle Dancer illustrated by Cornelius Van Wright and Ying-Hwa Hu. William Morrow & Co., 2000.

Rain Is Not My Indian Name illustrated by Lori Earley. HarperCollins, 2001.

Jingle Dancer Script

Chorus: *Tink, tink, tink, tink.*

Narrator One: Cone-shaped jingles sewn to Grandma Wolfe's dress sang.

Narrator Two: Every Grandma bounce-step brought clattering tinks as light blurred silver against jingles of tin.

Chorus: *Tink, tink, tink, tink.*

Narrator Three: Jenna daydreamed at the kitchen table, tasting honey on fry bread, her heart beating to the rhythm of the powwow drum.

Chorus: *Brum, brum, brum, brum.*

Narrator One: As Moon kissed Sun good night, Jenna shifted her head on Grandma Wolfe's shoulder.

Jenna: I want to jingle dance, too.

Grandma Wolfe: Next powwow, you could dance Girls. But we don't have enough time to mail-order tins for rolling jingles.

Narrator Two: Again and again, Jenna watched a videotape of Grandma Wolfe jingle dancing.

Narrator Three: When Grandma bounce-stepped on TV, Jenna bounce-stepped on family room carpet.

Narrator Two: But Jenna's dress would not be able to sing. It needed four rows of jingles.

Narrator One: As Sun fetched morning, Jenna danced east to Great-aunt Sis's porch. Jenna's bounce-steps crunched autumn leaves, but her steps didn't jingle.

Jenna:	Tell me the story about Bat.
Great-aunt Sis:	It is an old Muscogee story. Although other animals had said he was too small to make a difference, Bat won a ball game by flying high and catching a ball in his teeth.
Narrator Two:	Rising sunlight reached through a windowpane and flashed against …
Narrator Three:	What was it, hanging in Aunt Sis's bedroom?
Narrator One:	Jingles on a dress too long quiet.
Jenna:	May I borrow enough jingles to make a row?
Narrator Two:	Jenna did not want to take so many that Aunt Sis's dress would lose its voice.
Chorus:	*Tink, tink, tink, tink.*
Great-aunt Sis:	You may. My legs don't work so good anymore. Will you dance for me?
Narrator Three:	Jenna kissed Aunt Sis's cheek.
Jenna:	I will.
Narrator Two:	Now Jenna's dress needed three more rows.
Narrator One:	As Sun arrived at midcircle, Jenna skipped south to Mrs. Scott's brand-new duplex. At Jenna's side, jingles clinked.
Chorus:	*Tink, tink, tink, tink.*
Narrator Three:	Mrs. Scott led Jenna into the kitchen. Once again, Jenna rolled dough, and Mrs. Scott fried it.
Jenna:	May I borrow enough jingles to make a row?
Narrator Two:	Jenna did not want to take so many that Mrs. Scott's dress would lose its voice.
Mrs. Scott:	You may. At powwow, I'll be busy selling fry bread and Indian tacos. Will you dance for me?
Narrator Three:	Jenna gave Mrs. Scott a high five.
Jenna:	I will.
Narrator Two:	Now Jenna's dress needed two more rows.
Narrator One:	As Sun caught a glimpse of Moon, Jenna strolled west to Cousin Elizabeth's apartment. At Jenna's side, jingles clanked.

Chorus:	*Tink, tink, tink, tink.*
Narrator Three:	Elizabeth had arrived home late from the law firm. Once again, Jenna helped Elizabeth carry in her files.
Jenna:	May I borrow enough jingles to make a row?
Narrator Two:	Jenna did not want to take so many that Elizabeth's dress would lose its voice.
Cousin Elizabeth:	You may. This weekend, I'm working on a big case and can't go to powwow. Will you dance for me?
Narrator Three:	Jenna clasped her cousin's hands.
Jenna:	I will.
Narrator Two:	Now Jenna's dress needed one more row of jingles, but she didn't know which way to turn.
Narrator One:	As Moon glowed pale, Jenna shuffled north to Grandma Wolfe's.
Narrator Three:	At Jenna's side, jingles sat silent. High above, clouds wavered like worried ghosts.
Narrator Two:	When Jenna tugged open the door, jingles sang.
Chorus:	*Tink, tink, tink, tink.*
Narrator One:	Grandma Wolfe was jingle dancing on TV.
Narrator Two:	Jenna breathed in every "hey-ah-ho-o" of a powwow song. Her heart beat to the pounding of the drum.
Chorus:	*Brum, brum, brum, brum.*
Narrator Three:	On family room carpet, beaded moccasins waited for Jenna's feet.
Narrator One:	She shucked off a sneaker and slipped on a moccasin that long before had danced with Grandma Wolfe.
Narrator Two:	Jenna knew where to find her fourth row.
Jenna:	May I borrow enough jingles to make a row?
Narrator Two:	Jenna did not want to take so many that Grandma Wolfe's dress would lose its voice.
Narrator Three:	Grandma hugged Jenna.
Grandma Wolfe:	You may.

Narrator Two:	Now Jenna's dress could sing.
Narrator One:	Every night that week, Jenna helped Grandma Wolfe sew on jingles and bring together the dance regalia.
Narrator Two:	Every night, Jenna practiced her bounce-steps.
Narrator Three:	The drum sounded at the powwow the next weekend.
Chorus:	*Brum, brum, brum, brum.*
Narrator One:	As light blurred silver, Jenna jingle danced …
Great-aunt Sis:	… for me because my legs ache,
Mrs. Scott:	… for me while I sold fry bread,
Cousin Elizabeth:	… for me while I worked on my big case,
Grandma Wolfe:	… and for me.
Narrator Two:	Grandma Wolfe warmed Jenna like Sun.
Chorus:	*Tink, tink, tink, tink.*

The End

Jingle Dancer Activities

Art Connection

Jingle Dancing

In order to best understand the story told in *Jingle Dancer,* you will want students to know a bit about jingle dancing. After an initial reading of the book, ask students to contribute what they have learned about jingle dancing in the story. List student responses on the board or chart paper.

Now share with your students one or more of the following video resources that include jingle dancing:

- *Men's & Women's Native American Dance Styles, Volume I.* Full Circle Communications, 1993. (Purchase information at www.fullcir.com/pow wow.htm.)

- *New Dawn of Tradition: A Wisconsin Powwow.* Milwaukee Public Television, 1998. (Purchase information at www. ecb.org/education/tapedub.htm.)

After watching and learning more, add additional facts to your list. If possible, invite a group of jingle dancers to share this dance form with your students.

> **Arts Standards**
>
> **Dance**
>
> - Understands dance in various cultures and historical periods

Social Studies Connections

Four Directions

Jenna travels in four directions to visit female relatives and friends to ask for help in creating a dress with four rows of jingles. Explain to students that Cynthia Leitich Smith notes the direction that Jenna travels to each house.

Review maps and the directions on a compass. Some book resources that might be helpful include:

- *Mapping Penny's World* by Loreen Leedy. Henry Holt & Company, 2000.

- *Me on the Map* by Joan Sweeney, illustrated by Annette Cable. Crown Publishers, 1996.

As a group or individual activity, ask students to create a map of Jenna's neighborhood in the story, including the houses of Grandma Wolfe, Great-aunt Sis, Mrs. Scott, and Cousin Elizabeth in their proper places in relation to each other.

> **Geography Standards**
>
> **The World in Spatial Terms**
>
> - Understands the characteristics and uses of maps, globes, and other geographic tools and technologies

Community Members

Too often, American Indian cultures are taught as cultures of the past. Therefore,

one of the pleasures of sharing *Jingle Dancer* with students is the opportunity to remind them that Native peoples are part of the ongoing fabric of contemporary culture, living lives as active community members throughout North America.

Ask students to list evidence from the story that Jenna and the other characters live in contemporary America on the left side of the Community Member graphic organizer on page 51. Now discuss the blending of mainstream American life with Native cultural traditions and customs in *Jingle Dancer*. Ask students to list evidence from the story that Jenna and her community also enjoy Native cultural traditions. List them on the right side of the graphic organizer.

History Standards

Grades K–4 History: Topic 1—Living and Working Together in Families and Communities, Now and Long Ago

- Understands the history of a local community and how communities in North America varied long ago

---

Cultural Traditions

After completing the Community Members activity above, invite students to discuss their own cultural customs, often part of holidays or community celebrations. You may want to use the Cultural Traditions graphic organizer on page 52. Of course, it is important to be sensitive to cultural differences and to the fact that some students may be living in dual cultures or outside their biologically hereditary culture as a result of adoption, intermarriage, or com-

plex family patterns. The goal of this activity, however, is to celebrate a diversity of cultures in any community.

Help Needed!

When Jenna needs jingles to make her jingle dancing plan a reality, she turns to four members of her community, Great-aunt Sis, Mrs. Scott, Cousin Elizabeth, and Grandma Wolfe. Ask students to think of a plan they might need help with. Then ask them which four family or community members they would ask for help. Invite them to explain why they would choose each person on their list. Would each person give them a different type of help? Who would be the most helpful of all?

Behavior Studies Standards

- Understands that group and cultural influences contribute to human development, identity, and behavior

---

Language Arts Connections

Show, Don't Tell

A principal way that authors reveal important aspects of the characters in their stories, including cultural heritage, is through actions, or the things they do. Authors do this by following the "Show, Don't Tell" rule. As students complete the Community Members activity on page 48, they will understand how Cynthia Leitich Smith revealed Jenna's cultural identity through the things she and the other characters did.

After completing the Cultural Traditions activity, invite students to write a fictional

paragraph (or short story, depending on the age of your students) in which a contemporary character engages in one of the cultural customs on the Cultural Traditions graphic organizer (page 52). Encourage students to reveal the characters' cultural heritage by showing it as Cynthia Leitich Smith does in *Jingle Dancer*, rather than simply stating it.

Language Arts Standards

Writing

- Uses the stylistic and rhetorical aspects of writing

What Time Is It?

Cynthia Leitich Smith makes exciting use of metaphors to describe the time of day in *Jingle Dancer*. After introducing, or reviewing, metaphors with your students, create a list of the time-of-day metaphors in the story (for example, "As Moon kissed Sun good night"). For each, ask students to explain what time of day it is and what things are being compared. Use the What

Time Is It? graphic organizer on page 53 to record responses. Then invite students to create their own nature metaphors.

Language Arts Standards

Writing

- Uses the stylistic and rhetorical aspects of writing

The Story about Bat

In *Jingle Dancer*, Jenna asks Great-aunt Sis to tell the story about Bat. You may want to share the full story with your students. Share Joseph Bruchac's telling of this Creek legend with your students to enhance their study of *Jingle Dancer*.

- *The Great Ball Game: A Muskogee Story* by Joseph Bruchac, illustrated by Susan L. Roth. Dial, 1994.

Language Arts Standards

Reading

- Uses reading skills and strategies to understand and interpret a variety of literary texts

 # Community Member

Evidence of Contemporary Life	Evidence of Native Culture and Traditions

Cultural Traditions

Student Name	Culture	Tradition or Custom

What Time Is It?

METAPHOR	MEANING
What does the text say?	What time of day is it and what is being compared?
	What time is it?
	What time is it?
	What time is it?
	What time is it?
	What time is it?
	What time is it?

Mudball

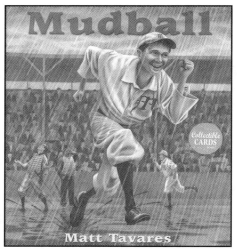

Read *Mudball* and the interview with Matt Tavares below to familiarize yourself with the book and the author. When you are ready to perform the script with your students, read the book aloud to the children so that they can enjoy the illustrations and become familiar with the story. Then, hand out a set of photocopied scripts to 17 children. Ask the remaining children to be the audience, or, if the class is small, assign all remaining children to the chorus. Have performers face the audience and simply read their parts on the first run-through. Once all readers are comfortable with their parts, have a second reading with the opportunity to use props or costumes, if desired, and to act out the story while reading. Your turn comes at the end—you read the Epilogue!

Meet Matt Tavares

Baseball. Christmas Eve. In his extraordinary artwork, Matt Tavares undertakes these well-loved subjects. His pencil and watercolor illustrations lend a nostalgic feel to these most nostalgic of themes, while his delightfully detailed imagery and dramatic lighting evoke a true sense of magic. Matt Tavares grew up surrounded by books and reading. From the time he was very young, his mother read to him every night, and his family made countless trips to the public library. Years later, as a junior in college, he rediscovered his love for picture books and decided to try to make his own. "I thought back to my own childhood, and tried to make a book that I would have liked when

I was a kid," he says. Now, as a successful author/illustrator, Matt Tavares lives with his wife and their daughter in Ogunquit, Maine.

***Mudball* is a story about the All-American sport of baseball. Looking over your body of work, one might assume that you are a baseball fan. How accurate is that assumption? Please share a bit about your personal history with the game.**

MT: It's true—I'm a huge baseball fan. The Red Sox are my team, but I enjoy watching any baseball game, whether it's the Red Sox

vs. the Yankees, or a minor league game. I grew up near Boston, and Fenway Park has always been one of my favorite places. As a child, I dreamed of someday playing for the Red Sox. As I got older, it became clear that I was much better at drawing than I was at baseball. But I still love watching the Sox, and I still have a great time playing softball every summer in my local league.

One of the great charms of this story is that Little Andy Oyler is such an underdog. He's short—the shortest man in the whole league—and he isn't much of a hitter, either. How did the character of Andy arise? Is he based on anyone you know?

MT: Andy Oyler was a real person, and I based some of his character on the few things I knew about him, like the fact that he wasn't a very good hitter and that he was pretty small for a baseball player. I also relied on my own experiences of playing and watching baseball. I remember days in high school and Little League when I just couldn't seem to get a hit, no matter how hard I tried. And just like Andy, there were times when I wanted to quit. So I know just how Andy must have felt when he was in the midst of his horrible slump.

Mudball **is very much a period piece and your narration is reminiscent of old-time radio broadcasts. How did you go about capturing the historic feel? Were there any particular things you read, listened to, or viewed?**

MT: I just tried to keep the text as simple as possible and describe the events in a way that someone would if they were watching them unfold in real time—much like a radio broadcaster. Originally, the text was much longer. But that slowed down the

pace of the story a bit. So I whittled it down until the book could be read at a pace that matched the urgency of the situation.

Interestingly, I really wasn't trying to make it sound like an old-time radio broadcast. One of the great things about baseball is its timelessness. Whether it happened in 1903 or 2003, the story of Andy Oyler's muddy home run would probably be described pretty much the same way.

I did plenty of historical research, but mostly for the pictures. I needed to make sure everything looked just as it would have looked back in 1903—from the players' uniforms, to the fans' clothes, to the ballpark itself. I found most of my information at the library and on the Internet. I think that the old-fashioned look of the pictures might help the text sound old-fashioned, too.

Please discuss your choice of secondary characters for the story. How did you choose which other players/participants to include? Are any of them based on real people?

MT: All of the players mentioned in *Mudball* were actually members of the 1903 Minneapolis Millers. I chose Maloney, Yeager, and McCreery as the three base runners because they were all starting players, and it seemed possible that they would have been on base when Andy was up. McCreery was the biggest power hitter on the team, so I gave him the nickname "Slugger." For the opposing team, I originally included the names of players who actually played for the St. Paul Saints in 1903, but that got very confusing. There were too many names to keep track of. It made more sense to just refer to those players by their position, and call them the pitcher, the catcher, the first baseman, etc.

Because you are both an author and illustrator, it would be interesting to know whether you began the creation of this book with images or text. Please talk about your process for this book and your creative process in general as regards art and text.

MT: For the most part, I write the text first then do the pictures. But there is always a lot of back and forth. Usually, my first draft is way too long, and I include lots of little details. Then once I decide what the pictures will be, I realize that I can delete some of the text, because a lot of the story will be told in the pictures. For example, in my book, *Zachary's Ball,* the story originally included a whole paragraph about how much Zachary loved baseball. But once I made the pictures, I realized that if I showed a scene in Zachary's room, and the reader could see all his baseball posters and memorabilia, it would be clear that he loved baseball and I could delete that whole paragraph. The same thing happened in *Mudball.* Once I drew the pictures, I took away a lot of the text that described the scene, because it was no longer needed.

How can readers learn more about you and your books?

MT: They can go to their local library and look for my books, or they can visit my Web site at www.matt-tavares.com.

Books by Matt Tavares

Mudball. Candlewick Press, 2005.

Oliver's Game. Candlewick Press, 2004.

This Place I Know: Poems of Comfort by Georgia Heard, illustrated by Eighteen Renowned Picture Book Artists (including Matt Tavares). Candlewick Press, 2002.

'Twas the Night Before Christmas: Or An Account of a Visit from St. Nicholas by Clement Clarke Moore, illustrated by Matt Tavares. Candlewick Press, 2002.

Zachary's Ball. Candlewick Press, 2000.

Mudball Script

Roles

Little Andy Oyler	Slugger McCreery	Second Baseman	Narrator One
Umpire	Catcher	Miller's Manager	Narrator Two
Maloney	First Baseman	Saints' Manager	Narrator Three
Yeager	Pitcher	Chorus (Three readers)	

Narrator One: One fateful spring day in 1903, Little Andy Oyler practiced his swing—and tried not to listen to the heckling fans of the opposing team, the St. Paul Saints.

Chorus: *(Shout.)* Hey, shorty! I bet you can't even hit it past the pitcher's mound!

Chorus: *(Sneer.)* Yeah! My grandmother can hit it farther than you!

Narrator Two: Andy wondered if maybe, just maybe, they were right. After all, he was the shortest player on his team, the Minneapolis Millers—and in the whole league.

Narrator Three: Even worse, he just couldn't seem to get a hit, no matter how hard he tried.

Narrator One: As a cold drizzle began to fall from the gray sky, Little Andy Oyler thought ...

Little Andy Oyler: Maybe it's time for me to quit.

Narrator Two: The Minneapolis Millers trailed the St. Paul Saints by three runs.

Narrator Three: They were down to their final out, the bases were loaded and Little Andy Oyler was their only hope.

Narrator One: But just as he stepped into the batter's box, it began to pour.

Umpire: *(Yell.)* Time out! Wait until this storm cloud passes!

Narrator Two: But the rain kept coming, and within minutes the infield had turned to mud and the field was spotted with puddles.

Narrator Three:	Finally, the umpire yelled ...
Umpire:	*(Yell.)* Play on!
Narrator Three:	He was hoping for one quick out, and with Little Andy Oyler up, he knew the chances of that were good.
Narrator One:	Andy's cold hands trembled as he tightened his grip on the bat. Maloney took his lead off first.
Maloney:	Bring us home, kid!
Narrator Two:	Yeager stood ankle-deep in a puddle, just left of second base.
Yeager:	*(Yell.)* Just keep your eye on the ball!
Narrator Three:	Slugger McCreery wrung out his jersey at third.
Slugger McCreery:	*(Growl.)* And whatever you do, don't strike out!
Narrator One:	The pitcher wound up and fired a fastball. But the wet ball slipped as it left his hand, and went hurtling straight toward Little Andy Oyler's head.
Maloney:	*(Yell.)* Look out!
Narrator Two:	Yeager covered his eyes.
Yeager:	*(Scream.)* Duck!
Slugger McCreery:	*(Shout.)* And don't strike out!
Narrator Three:	Andy braced himself. But just when he expected the ball to hit him, he heard the unmistakable sound of ball against bat.
Chorus:	CRACK!
Narrator One:	Somehow, Andy's bat had hit the ball. Everybody heard it ...
Narrator Two:	but nobody saw where it went.
Narrator Three:	Little Andy Oyler took off for first.
Narrator One:	The catcher ran in circles around home plate, ready to catch the ball when it fell from the sky.
Catcher:	*(Shout.)* He popped it up! I saw the ball go straight up!
Narrator Two:	He ran in circles around home plate, ready to catch the ball when it fell from the sky.
Chorus:	But it never did.

   © 2006 by Toni Buzzeo (UpstartBooks)

First Baseman: (*Shout.*) I think it's in this puddle! I saw it land right here!

Narrator Three: The catcher splashed and splashed, but still the ball was nowhere to be found.

Narrator One: Meanwhile, Slugger McCreery strutted across home plate. The score was 3 to 1.

Chorus: (*Yell.*) Oyler stole the ball! Check his pockets!

Narrator Two: Andy raced toward second, but the second baseman stood in his way.

Second Baseman: (*Growl.*) Come here, you little thief!

Narrator Three: The second baseman dove, but Andy jumped right over him.

Narrator One: He rounded second and headed for third as Yeager slid safely home. The score was 3 to 2.

Narrator Two: The pitcher screamed at the catcher.

Pitcher: (*Scream.*) What'd you do with the ball?

Catcher: (*Yell.*) I didn't do anything! It just disappeared!

Narrator Three: As they were arguing, Maloney slid between them and crossed home plate.

Narrator One: The score was tied.

Narrator Two: Andy tagged third and headed for home—but the muddy second baseman was hot on his trail.

Second Baseman: I'm gonna get you!

Narrator Three: With every step, the second baseman drew closer and closer.

Narrator One: But just as he was ready to pounce on Andy—

Narrator Two: he tripped and fell facedown in the mud.

Narrator Three: Little Andy Oyler crossed home plate with the winning run.

Narrator One: The Millers' manager yelled at the Saints' manager.

Millers' Manager: (*Yell.*) We scored four runs! We win!

Narrator One: The Saints' manager shouted at the Millers' manager.

Saints' Manager: (*Shout.*) It doesn't count! Nobody knows where the ball went!

Second Baseman: *(Moan.)* Aaugh! I tripped on a rock and twisted my ankle.

Narrator Two: The umpire scratched his head.

Umpire: There weren't any rocks when I raked the field this morning.

Second Baseman: Oh yeah? Then what's this?

Narrator Three: The umpire grabbed the ball from the second baseman's hand.

Umpire: *(Shout.)* Fair ball! The Millers win!

Narrator One: The Millers jumped for joy.

Narrator Two: The fans rushed the field.

Narrator Three: And everyone crowded around Little Andy Oyler—the big hero of Minneapolis.

The End

Epilogue

Even though his home run traveled only a few feet in front of home plate, it seemed to break Andy Oyler out of his slump. He had three hits the next day, and by the end of the season, he was one of the Minneapolis Millers' best players.

The St. Paul Saints fans kept making fun of Andy for being short, but it didn't bother him one bit. He knew that he didn't have to hit the ball over the fence to help his team—he just had to play hard and have fun. And that's what Andy Oyler did, even on days when he couldn't seem to get a hit, no matter how hard he tried. Andy loved playing for the Millers, and the fans at Nicollet Park loved watching him play.

Andy Oyler never did hit another home run. But while other records have come and gone, no player has come close to doing what he did on that muddy day back in 1903, when the shortest player in the league became a hero by hitting the shortest home run in baseball history.

Mudball Activities

Language Arts Connection

Baseball Lingo

Matt Tavares fills *Mudball* with the language of baseball. As you read the book, invite students to identify each baseball word, term, or phrase. After building a list, invite students to create a Baseball Lingo Dictionary, using the Baseball Lingo graphic organizer on page 65. For each word, term, or phrase, ask students to supply a dictionary definition (when available), create an illustration, quote it as Matt Tavares used it in *Mudball,* and use it in an original sentence.

For additional definitions beyond the general dictionary, you might want to use the "Baseball and Physics Dictionary" available on the ThinkQuest Web site at <u>library. thinkquest.org/11902/cgi-bin/allterms. html</u>.

<u>**Language Arts Standards**</u>

Writing

- Uses the general skill and strategies of the writing process

- Uses the stylistic and rhetorical aspects of writing

Reading

- Uses the general skills and strategies of the reading process

- Uses reading skills and strategies to understand and interpret a variety of literary texts

- Uses reading skills and strategies to understand and interpret a variety of informational texts

Social Studies Connections

Back in Time

Mudball opens with the line: "One fateful spring day in 1903, Little Andy Oyler practiced his swing—and tried not to listen to the heckling fans of the opposing team, the St. Paul Saints." The story takes place a little over a hundred years ago. Re-read the story to students and ask them to notice, in both the text and the illustrations, hints that the story takes place long ago. (**Note:** Sports fans in your group will likely supply you with quite a long list!) Now complete the One Hundred Years Ago graphic organizer on page 66. Ask students to consider how the text and illustrations would have been different if Matt Tavares had been writing and illustrating a contemporary story. If, by the end of the activity, none of your students have mentioned the book being rendered primarily in sepia tones, ask them to speculate on this decision on Tavares's part.

<u>**History Standards**</u>

Grades K–4: Topic 1—Living and Working Together in Families and Communities, Now and Long Ago

- Understands the history of a local community and how communities in North America varied long ago

One Hundred Years Ago in Books

Once you've made a list of the items author/illustrator Matt Tavares included in the book to make it authentic to the time,

you might want to further explore America one hundred years ago. Invite students to take a trip back in time through books.

First, in addition to *Mudball*, share other books with students that detail life in 1900, either factually or through fiction. A few interesting titles include:

- *Children of Long Ago: Poems* by Lessie Jones Little, illustrated by Jan Spivey Gilchrist. Philomel Books, 1988

- *Country Mouse Cottage: How We Lived One Hundred Years Ago* by Brooks Nigel, illustrated by Abigail Horner. Walker & Co., 2000.

- *Hattie and the Wild Waves* by Barbara Cooney, illustrated by R. Haynes. Viking, 1990.

- *House, House* by Jane Yolen, photographs by Jason Stemple. Marshall Cavendish, 1998.

- *If You Lived 100 Years Ago* by Ann McGovern, illustrated by Anna DiVito. Scholastic, 1999.

- *Old Home Day* by Donald Hall, illustrated by Emily Arnold McCully. Browndeer Press, 1996.

A more extensive bibliography can be found online at Nancy Keane's Children's Literature Web page at nancykeane.com/rl/294.htm.

History Standards

Grades K–4: Topic 1—Living and Working Together in Families and Communities, Now and Long Ago

- Understands family life now and in the past, and family life in various places long ago

- Understands the history of a local community and how communities in North America varied long ago

Language Arts Standards

Reading

- Uses the general skills and strategies of the reading process

- Uses reading skills and strategies to understand and interpret a variety of literary texts

- Uses reading skills and strategies to understand and interpret a variety of informational texts

One Hundred Years Ago Online

Explore America one hundred years ago with your students online. To learn more about technology in 1900, begin with the PBS Web site at pbskids.org/wayback/tech1900. Then explore what schools were like one hundred years ago on the ThinkQuest Web site at library.thinkquest.org/J002606/early1900s.html.

You will find photographs and information about entertainment and leisure in American one hundred years ago on the American Memory Web site at memory.loc.gov/ammem/awlhtml/awlleis.html.

Finally, after reading books in the One Hundred Years Ago in Books activity above, ask students to draw conclusions about how life has changed in the intervening one hundred years and record them on the One Hundred Years Ago graphic organizer (page 66).

Mathematics Connections

How Much Did it Cost?

The economics of living in the United States has changed considerably in the time since Little Andy Oyler was playing ball for the Minneapolis Millers. One hundred years ago, people were paid less, but prices were also much lower. Explore information about prices and wages online at the Morris County (New Jersey) Library Web site, www.gti.net/mocolib1/prices/1902.html.

Invite students to investigate the comparable prices of products as reported for 1902 and as they are today. (**Note:** Bring in stacks of advertisements from your local paper for department stores, grocery stores, drugstores, car dealerships, and others.) Create a set of classroom charts by types of products. On each, list individual products, their prices in 1902, and their prices today.

Of course, this isn't meaningful information without also exploring the differences in wages between the two eras. Information about wages at the turn of the century can be found at www.chipublib.org/004chicago/1900/fam.html.

However, in general, the average wage in 1900 was $.22 an hour, or $12.74 weekly. Ask students to compare this to current average weekly wages. Explain that these vary by geographic area and types of jobs, with New York County, New York, having an average weekly wage of $2,025 per week and Cameron County, Texas, having the lowest national average weekly wage of $460 per week.

With older students, discuss whether wages and prices have gone up at a comparable rate.

Baseball Statistics

Little Andy Oyler, as Matt Tavares mentions in his interview, was a real player for the Minneapolis Millers in 1903. In fact, statistics for Oyler and his team for 1903 are

online at stewthornley.net/millers_1901_1910.html#1903.

Ask students to look at the statistics for the 1903 Minneapolis Millers and answer the following questions:

- Which four players played in the most games?

- How many total games did those players play in?

- What was the Millers' home run total for the season?

- Which player hit the most home runs?

- Put the pitchers in order by their number of losses rather than their number of wins.

Baseball Lingo

Word, Term, or Phrase:	
Definition:	
Sentence in *Mudball*:	
Original sentence:	

One Hundred Years Ago

Category	100 Years Ago	Today
Houses		
Jobs		
Roles of Men and Women		
School		
Clothing		
Transportation		
Technology		
Entertainment		

Old Cricket

Read *Old Cricket* and the interview with Lisa Wheeler below to familiarize yourself with the book and the author. Once you are ready to perform the script with your students, read the book aloud to the children so that they can enjoy the illustrations and become familiar with the story. Then, hand out a set of photocopied scripts to 11 children. Ask the remaining children to be the audience. Have performers face the audience and simply read their parts on the first run-through. Once all readers are comfortable with their parts, have a second reading with the opportunity to use props or costumes, if desired, and to act out the story while reading.

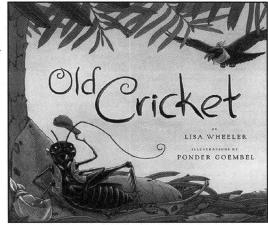

Meet Lisa Wheeler

Lisa Wheeler is passionate about children's books. "I love everything about them, including the smell," she says. To date, Lisa has 16 titles on bookstore shelves, with eight more to follow over the next few years. She's written picture books in prose and in rhyme, an easy reader series, two books of poems, and creative nonfiction for the very young. Her upcoming titles include *Hokey Pokey: Another Prickly Love Story* illustrated by Janie Bynum, *Mammoths on the Move* illustrated by Kurt Cyrus, and *Castaway Cats* illustrated by Ponder Goembel. Lisa shares her Michigan home with one husband, two dogs, three kids, and an assortment of anthropomorphic characters.

Old Cricket very much has the feel of an oral story, which makes it perfect for reader's theater. What was the origin of this story?

LW: We lived in the same little house for 16 years, and right outside my bedroom window was a bush. In that bush lived a cricket that liked to chirp—loudly—every summer. It probably wasn't the same cricket year after year, but in my mind I pictured him as an old cricket. Many nights I would be wakened from sleep because he wouldn't stop cricking. So I decided I would write his story, and then maybe he would be quiet and let me get some sleep.

One of the many entertaining aspects of this story is your language. How did you go about choosing the ear-pleasing vocabulary for *Old Cricket?*

LW: Well, I always heard his song as crick-crick-crick, so that part was easy. I knew this cricket was cranky, because he apparently never slept, so all those lovely "C" words just kept presenting themselves. Cricket, crow, cantankerous, crotchety, crumb, creak and even "crook in her finger" were perfect for the story. I do love alliteration!

Old Cricket is a crafty old character. What or who was your inspiration for his character?

LW: I loved Aesop's Fables when I was a kid and read them over and over again. I didn't know it when I was writing this book, but I believe *Old Cricket* was heavily influenced by Aesop. I dedicated the book to my in-laws, because once the art was complete, Old Cricket and his Missus looked so much like my husband's parents that I was able to see how they influenced the story's directions as well—they were always doing home improvement projects and my father-in-law was usually on a ladder.

There is a long tradition in literature of "trickster tales." How does *Old Cricket* fit into this tradition?

LW: I never set out to write a trickster tale, so when reviewers and educators started describing it as such, I was surprised. I'd always viewed trickster tales as being Native American stories. But a trickster is a trickster, and Old Cricket certainly tried to pull a fast one.

You write so many humorous books for children that kids love. What draws you to writing funny books?

LW: My goal as a writer is to entertain. When I was a child, my favorite books were ones that took me away from my troubles and let me be happy and carefree, if only for a few minutes. I love to hear kids laugh when they read my books. I love to hear their parents and teachers laugh as well. Some writers are good at making people think deep thoughts and some are good at making people get sentimental and weepy. I prefer to crack people up.

I think my funniest book is *Turk and Runt.* I cannot read that book without laughing myself. I tell kids that when I am writing, I have to crack myself up. If I am not laughing at my jokes, chances are my reader won't be. My other funniest (to me) are *Wool Gathering: A Sheep Family Reunion,* the Fitch & Chip series, *Farmer Dale's Red Pickup Truck* and *Porcupining.*

How can readers learn more about you and your books?

LW: They can go to my Web site at www. lisawheelerbooks.com. There, they will find activities to accompany my books. Everything from coloring pages to Teacher's Guides are free to print out.

Books by Lisa Wheeler

Avalanche Annie: A Not-So-Tall Tale illustrated by Kurt Cyrus. Harcourt, 2003.

Bubble Gum, Bubble Gum illustrated by Laura Huliska-Beith. Little, Brown, and Company, 2004.

Castaway Cats illustrated by Ponder Goembel. Simon & Schuster, 2006.

Farmer Dale's Red Pickup Truck illustrated by Ivan Bates. Harcourt, 2004.

Hokey Pokey: Another Prickly Love Story illustrated by Janie Bynum. Little, Brown, and Company, 2005.

Invasion of the Pig Sisters (Fitch and Chip) illustrated by Frank Ansley. Simon & Schuster, 2005.

Mammoths on the Move illustrated by Kurt Cyrus. Harcourt, 2005.

New Pig in Town (Fitch and Chip) illustrated by Frank Ansley. Simon & Schuster, 2003.

Old Cricket illustrated by Ponder Goembel. Simon & Schuster, 2003.

One Dark Night illustrated by Ivan Bates. Harcourt, 2003.

Porcupining illustrated by Janie Bynum. Little, Brown, and Company, 2002.

Sailor Moo: Cow at Sea illustrated by Ponder Goembel. Simon & Schuster, 2002.

Seadogs: An Epic Ocean Operetta illustrated by Mark Siegel. Simon & Schuster, 2004.

Sixteen Cows illustrated by Kurt Cyrus. Harcourt, 2002.

Te Amo, Bebé, Little One illustrated by Maribel Suárez. Little, Brown, and Company, 2004.

Turk and Runt: A Thanksgiving Comedy illustrated by Frank Ansley. Simon & Schuster, 2002.

Uncles and Antlers illustrated by Brian Floca. Simon & Schuster, 2004.

When Pigs Fly (Fitch and Chip) illustrated by Frank Ansley. Simon & Schuster, 2003.

Who's Afraid of Granny Wolf? (Fitch and Chip) illustrated by Frank Ansley. Simon & Schuster, 2004.

Wool Gathering: A Sheep Family Reunion illustrated by Frank Ansley. Simon & Schuster, 2001.

Old Cricket Script

Narrator One: Old Cricket woke up feeling cranky.

Narrator Two: And crotchety.

Narrator Three: And cantankerous.

Narrator One: So when his Missus asked him to ready their roof for winter, he came up with a clever plan.

Chorus: You don't get to be an *old* cricket by being a dumb bug.

Old Cricket: Consarn it! I woke with a creak in my knee, dear wife. I can't be climbing rooftops today.

Missus Cricket: Well, hobble yourself over to see Doc Hopper.

Narrator Two: She bundled up a bit of breakfast for him to eat along the way.

Narrator Three: Old Cricket took his bundle and left the house.

Chorus: Creak-creak-creak!

Narrator Three: Just in case his Missus was watching.

Narrator One: He hadn't gone far when he came upon his cousin, Katydid, who was picking berries off a bush for winter.

Cousin Katydid: Good to see you, Cousin. Have you come to help me pick berries?

Narrator Two: Old Cricket, still feeling cranky, didn't want to help.

Narrator One: So he came up with a clever plan.

Chorus: You don't get to be an *old* cricket by being a dumb bug.

Old Cricket:	I wish I could. But I woke with a creak in my knee and a crick in my neck, so I can't pick berries today. I'm off to see Doc Hopper.
Cousin Katydid:	That's too bad. Here, have a berry to munch along the way.
Narrator Two:	Old Cricket packed the berry in his bundle with his breakfast.
Narrator Three:	Then he wobbled off.
Chorus:	Creak-creak-creak! Crick-crick-crick!
Narrator Three:	Just in case Cousin Katydid was watching.
Narrator One:	When the sun was high in the sky, Old Cricket saw his neighbors, the Ants, in their field. They were bringing in the last of the corn.
Uncle Ant:	Wonderful to see you. Have you come to help with the harvest?
Narrator Two:	Old Cricket, still feeling crotchety, didn't want to help.
Narrator One:	So he came up with a clever plan.
Chorus:	You don't get to be an *old* cricket by being a dumb bug.
Old Cricket:	I'm sorry. But I woke with a creak in my knee, a crick in my neck, and a crack in my back. I can't haul corn today. I'm off to see Doc Hopper.
Uncle Ant:	That's too bad. Here, take a small kernel to nibble along the way.
Narrator Two:	Old Cricket packed the kernel into his bundle with his berry and his breakfast.
Narrator Three:	Then he dawdled off.
Chorus:	Creak-creak-creak! Crick-crick-crick! Crack-crack-crack!
Narrator Three:	Just in case Uncle Ant was watching.
Narrator One:	Now Old Cricket, tired from carrying the bulging bundle but feeling rather pleased with his clever self, had no intention of going to see Doc Hopper.

Narrator Two:	Instead, he settled under a piney shrub and soon fell fast asleep.
Narrator One:	He was awakened by Old Crow, who came calling at mealtime.
Old Crow:	Caw-caw-caw! Have you come to be my lunch?
Narrator Two:	Old Cricket, still feeling rather cantankerous, didn't want to be Old Crow's lunch.
Narrator One:	So he came up with a clever plan.
Chorus:	You don't get to be an *old* cricket by being a dumb bug.
Old Cricket:	I'm sorry. But I woke with a creak in my knee, a crick in my neck, a crack in my back, and a hic-hic-hiccup in my head. I'd surely go bouncing around in your belly if you ate me up today.
Narrator Three:	Then Old Cricket started off.
Chorus:	Creak-creak-creak! Crick-crick-crick! Crack-crack-crack! Hic-hic-hic!
Narrator Three:	Because he knew Old Crow was watching.
Narrator One:	But Old Crow was not tricked.
Chorus:	You don't get to be an *old* crow by being a birdbrain.
Narrator Two:	In a single swoop he snuck up behind Old Cricket, and …
Old Crow:	CAW!
Narrator Two:	… scared some real hiccups right into that dumb bug.
Old Crow:	Now be a good lunch and hold still.
Narrator Three:	Holding still was the last thing Old Cricket wanted to do. With his bundle on his back, he hightailed it towards home.
Chorus:	Hic-hic-hic! Caw-caw-caw!
Narrator Three:	… close behind.
Narrator One:	Hurrying back through the now-empty field, he slipped on strands of corn silk and … WHACK … got a crack in his back.

Old Cricket: Cornsakes!

Narrator One: Old Cricket struggled to his feet.

Narrator Two: But just before Old Crow could snatch him up, Old Cricket reached in his bundle, pulled out the corn kernel, and tossed it.

Narrator Three: Old Crow caught the kernel, but kept on coming.

Narrator One: Old Cricket ran.

Chorus: Hic-hic-hic!
Crack-crack-crack!
Caw-caw-caw!

Narrator One: … close behind.

Narrator Two: Scurrying past the now-empty berry bush, he stumbled on a stick and … THWICK … got a crick in his neck.

Old Cricket: Crikey!

Narrator One: Old Cricket scrambled to get away.

Narrator Two: But before Old Crow could gobble him down, Old Cricket reached into his bundle, plucked out the berry, and tossed it.

Narrator Three: Old Crow caught the berry, but kept on coming.

Narrator One: Old Cricket ran.

Chorus: Hic-hic-hic!
Crack-crack-crack!
Crick-crick-crick!
Caw-caw-caw!

Narrator One: … close behind.

Narrator Two: Now Old Cricket's bundle was nearly empty. The only thing left was his bit of breakfast, which, as it turned out, was nothing more than a dry piece of biscuit, no bigger than a crumb.

Old Cricket: Criminy!

Narrator Three: Old Cricket tossed the crumb.

Old Cricket: I am surely doomed.

Narrator Three: Old Crow caught the crumb in midair.

Narrator One: Old Cricket kept on running.

Chorus: Hic-hic-hic!
Crack-crack-crack!
Crick-crick-crick!
And now a creak-creak-creak came from his weary knees.
But there was no caw-caw-caw …

Narrator One: … close behind.

Narrator Two: Instead, there came a new sound.

Old Crow: Caw-caw-cough!

Narrator Three: That crumb had caught smack in the middle of Old Crow's throat!

Narrator One: Old Cricket never slowed as he looked back to see Old Crow, in a flurry of feathers, shaking his claw and caw-caw-coughing his fool head off.

Narrator Two: And as luck would have it, Old Cricket ran himself out right in front of Doc Hopper's doorway.

Narrator Three: Doc Hopper fixed each creak, each crick, each crack, and each hic. Then he sent Old Cricket on home where …

Narrator One: … his Missus was waiting with a crook in her finger as she pointed her clever husband toward their sagging rooftop.

Chorus: 'Cause you don't get to be an *old* Missus by being a dumb bug.

The End

Old Cricket Activities

Science Connections

It's a Buggy World

Old Cricket, Katydid, the Ants (including Uncle Ant), and Doc Hopper are all insects that share a single habitat, which is essential to the story of Old Cricket. Challenge students to research insects in the library media center in order to find three other insects that might share Old Cricket's habitat and could also have been included in the story. For each type of insect, ask students to record:

- Where it lives.

- What it does.

- What it eats.

- What it might have been "named" if included as a character in *Old Cricket*.

> **Science Standards**
>
> **Life Sciences**
>
> - Understands relationships among organisms and their physical environment

Home Improvement

Humans spend a great deal of time creating and caring for their homes in order to stay safe from the elements of nature. Animals—even insects—must do the same thing! In fact, the need for home improvement is what incites the story in *Old Cricket*. Missus Cricket wants Old Cricket to "ready the roof for winter." Ask students what sort of work this would require.

Then invite students to research a variety of insects and the types of homes they live in. What sorts of home improvement might each of these homes require?

> **Science Standards**
>
> **Life Sciences**
>
> - Understands relationships among organisms and their physical environment

Social Studies Connections

Community Cooperation

As the *Old Cricket* story unfolds, each of the insects is preparing for winter. Begin by asking students to review the actions each insect is taking to get ready. Then invite them to turn their thoughts to preparations of some sort in their community, whether seasonal or for some other annual event such as an "Old Home Days" parade or a holiday gift or food drive.

While Old Cricket was not a cooperative community member and had to be tricked into even participating in readying his own home for winter, emphasize the value of cooperation in communities to bring about safety or happiness in the community. Ask students to brainstorm and then select a project in their own community in which they might participate. Invite someone to come speak to the students about the various functions necessary to make the event a success and the role they might play.

Discuss the way each event on Old Cricket's journey causes another set of events. Ask students to speculate about what might have happened in each encounter to change the course of the story.

Language Arts Connections

The Story Unfolds

Old Cricket is a complicated story, carefully assembled from a cast of characters, their requests, corresponding responses, and resulting actions.

• The story begins when Old Cricket's wife asks him to repair the roof.

• Old Cricket replies he has a bad knee.

• She responds by sending him to Doc Hopper and giving him some breakfast.

• Old Cricket creak-creak-creaks off.

In order to better appreciate the story, have students create a chronological story map using The Story Unfolds graphic organizer on page 78.

• Who does Old Cricket encounter next?

• What does that character ask him to do?

• How does Old Cricket respond?

• What does the new character give Old Cricket?

• How does Old Cricket proceed on his way?

Satisfying Synonyms

Old Cricket opens with an alliterative set of synonyms for the word crabby:

> Old Cricket woke up
> feeling cranky.
> And crotchety.
> And cantankerous.

After discussing synonyms with your students, invite them, in groups of three or four, to come up with sets of synonyms for character traits that an author might use to describe a character or his or her mood as Lisa Wheeler did to describe Old Cricket. Challenge them to make as many of their synonyms as possible alliterative. Provide each group with a thesaurus and ask them to use the Satisfying Synonyms graphic organizer on page 79 to record their results. To further their understanding of the nuances of word meanings, ask them to use the dictionary to define each of the synonyms they choose.

Bug Life

With the exception of Old Crow, Old Cricket and the other characters in the story are all insects. One memorable way to enhance your students' learning about insects, including their understanding of insect habitat, behavior, and feeding, is to ask students to write a new version of *Old Cricket* using another set of insects. After completing the It's a Buggy World activity on page 75, challenge your students to rewrite *Old Cricket*. Students may wish to use Old Cricket as the main character again, or they may wish to research and create a new main character.

Before beginning, emphasize to students that even in fictional stories such as Old Cricket, the factual information about animal characters is often true. Therefore, researching the insect characters they have decided to include in their new version will be one of the keys to a satisfying story.

To extend the challenge for more able learners, invite them to move the habitat to a pond, the desert, or the rain forest!

Language Arts Standards

Writing

- Uses the stylistic and rhetorical aspects of writing

- Gathers and uses information for research purposes

Reading

- Uses reading skills and strategies to understand and interpret a variety of informational texts

Aphorisms

Lisa Wheeler wraps her story around the aphorism, "You don't get to be an *old cricket* by being a dumb bug." After sharing the book with students, discuss what they think this aphorism means. Explain that an aphorism is a brief, punchy statement of opinion or truth, which may embody a moral.

Gather a set of aphorisms to post on chart paper around the library or classroom. One at a time, discuss the meaning or truth inherent in each aphorism and invite students to collect their favorites into a booklet they can share with their families.

A good online adult resource for aphorisms is Aphorisms or 'Universal Truths' at www.theotherpages.org/quote-13.html.

Two books of aphorisms (also written for adults) are:

The Oxford Book of Aphorisms by John Gross. Oxford University Press, 2003.

The World in a Phrase: A History of Aphorisms by James Geary. Bloomsbury, 2005.

Language Arts Standards

Reading

- Uses reading skills and strategies to understand and interpret a variety of literary texts

The Story Unfolds

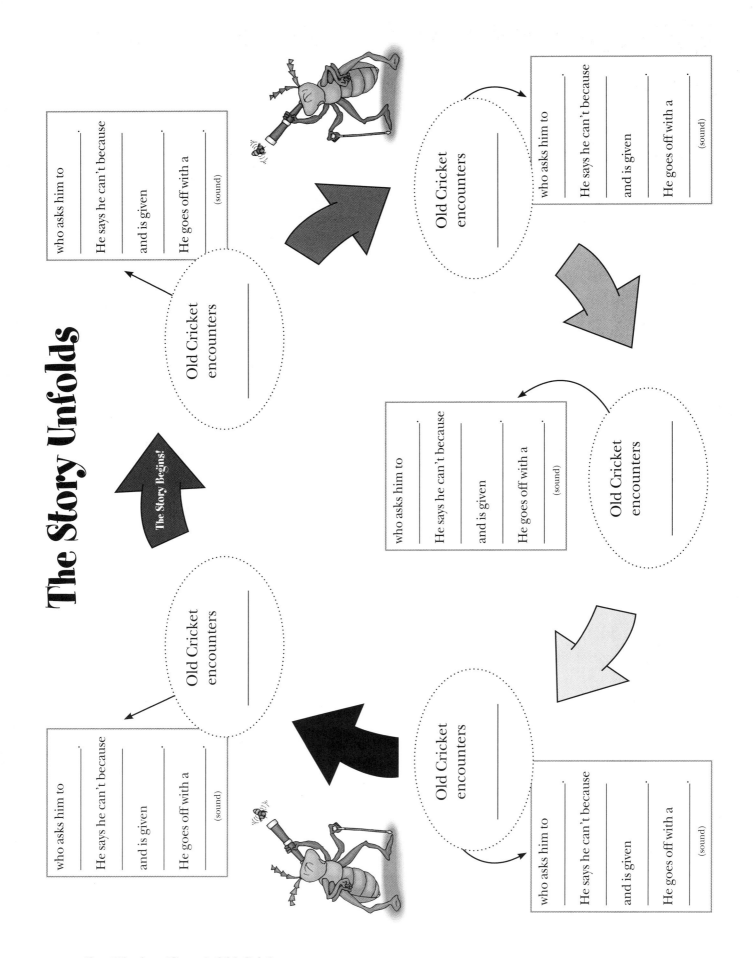

The Story Begins!

Old Cricket encounters ____

who ____ asks him to

He says he can't because ____

and is given ____

He goes off with a ____
(sound)

Read! Perform! Learn! Old Cricket   © 2006 by Toni Buzzeo (UpstartBooks)

Satisfying Synonyms

On the smaller circles, list three synonyms for the adjective in the center. In each of the larger circles, write the dictionary definition of the synonym.

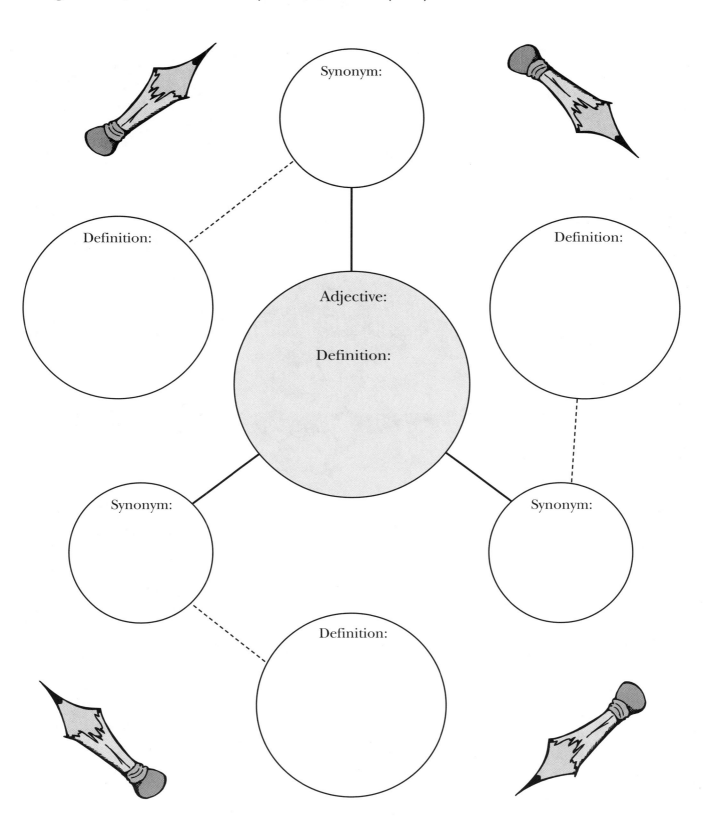

Synonym:

Definition:

Definition:

Adjective:

Definition:

Synonym:

Synonym:

Definition:

Rain Romp

Read *Rain Romp* and the interview with Jane Kurtz below to familiarize yourself with the book and the author. Once you are ready to perform the script with your students, read the book aloud to the children so that they can enjoy the illustrations and become familiar with the story. Then, hand out a set of photocopied scripts to nine children. Ask the remaining children to be the audience. Have performers face the audience and simply read their parts on the first run-through. (Select one of your strong readers as Narrator One. If this reader is a boy, change the personal pronouns of the three Chorus lines that use "her.") Once all readers are comfortable with their parts, have a second reading with the opportunity to use props or costumes, if desired, and to act out the story while reading.

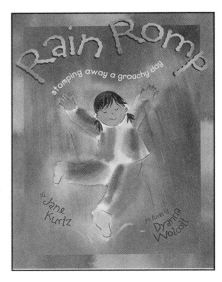

Meet Jane Kurtz

Since 1994, Jane Kurtz has published 20 books—nonfiction books, professional books for teachers, picture books, and novels that draw on her own childhood memories of growing up in Ethiopia, on living through the Red River flood of 1997, on her great grandmother's adventures traveling the Oregon Trail, and on the minor crises of her children's lives (from a friendship gone sour to the grouchiness of a rainy day). Her books have gathered accolades, starred reviews, and awards. A former elementary, secondary, and university teacher, Jane is a frequent and popular visitor to schools around the world and is the co-founder of the first free library for children in Addis Ababa, Ethiopia.

Rain Romp **is quite different from many of your other picture books. What was your inspiration for** *Rain Romp*? **Do you have a personal connection to the story?**

JK: In 1997, my family and I went through a tough time when a flood hit Grand Forks, North Dakota, where we were living. After the Red River went back within its banks, it seemed as if everyone in the city was mad and sad. Our house was torn down to make room for the new dike, and for a while, we lived in one of the trailers that the Federal Emergency

Management Agency provided. One gray morning, I was driving my grouchy daughter to school when the first lines of *Rain Romp* popped into my head.

What were you like as a child? Were you ever a howling, growling wolverine?

JK: Unfortunately for me, my older sister was naturally good and responsible and always seemed to do the right thing. As a second child, I was much more likely to let my frustrations get the better of me. Whenever I complained about my own children's behavior, my mom was happy to point out that I wasn't a very easy child to get along with, myself.

You grew up in Ethiopia where the weather is very different from the weather here in the United States. Please tell us about Ethiopian weather and what role it played in your life and games as a child.

JK: Ethiopia has two major seasons—rainy and dry. During the rainy season, it's not unusual to get a drenching downpour every day. While it rained, my sisters and I loved to climb into the attic of our house and create long stories about the families we cut out from the Sears catalogs my mom brought from the U.S. Crackling wood fires made the house with its mud walls and tin roof a cozy place. After the rain stopped, we could invent all kinds of games with the puddles.

Your language in this book is quite poetic, sometimes rhyming, sometimes metered, resulting in a charming read-aloud. Can you tell us more about the process of writing this book?

JK: I spent a lot of time reading aloud when I was a girl. My sisters and I also memorized our favorite poems and made a game out of seeing whether we could say the long ones from beginning to end. Some people play music "by ear" instead of by looking at notes. I always feel that I write by ear, listening to the sounds and rhythms of words—and sometimes my stories end up with a strong sense of rhythm and/or rhyme.

Does *Rain Romp* have connections with any of your other picture books?

JK: It might be interesting for young readers to compare *Rain Romp* with two of my other picture books—*Do Kangaroos Wear Seat Belts?* and *Water Hole Waiting*. All three have a strong sense of rhythm and rhyme. Another good connection is my picture book *River Friendly, River Wild*, about the Red River Flood of 1997. Looking especially at the poem "Mad" in that book, readers might want to ask how the girl narrator in both books is similar (and different).

How can readers learn more about you and your books?

JK: I speak in schools and at conferences all over the U.S., so maybe some of your readers will meet me in person some day. A good way to meet the virtual me is to visit my Web site at www.janekurtz.com.

Books by Jane Kurtz

American Southwest Resource Book: The People, Vol. 1. Eakin Press, 1996.

Bicycle Madness illustrated by Beth Peck. Henry Holt & Company, 2003.

Do Kangaroos Wear Seat Belts? illustrated by Jane K. Manning. Penguin, 2005.

Ethiopia: The Roof of Africa. Silver Burdett Press, 1991.

Faraway Home illustrated by E. B. Lewis. Harcourt, 2000.

The Feverbird's Claw. HarperCollins, 2004.

Fire on the Mountain illustrated by E. B. Lewis. Simon & Schuster, 1994.

I'm Sorry, Almira Ann illustrated by Susan Havice. Henry Holt & Company, 1999.

In the Small, Small Night illustrated by Rachel Isadora. Greenwillow Books, 2005.

Jakarta Missing. Greenwillow Books, 2001.

Johnny Appleseed illustrated by Mary Haverfield. Aladdin, 2004.

Memories of Sun: Stories of Africa and America. HarperCollins, 2004.

Miro in the Kingdom of the Sun illustrated by David Frampton. Houghton Mifflin, 1996.

Mister Bones: Dinosaur Hunter illustrated by Mary Haverfield. Aladdin Books, 2004.

Only a Pigeon illustrated by E. B. Lewis. Simon & Schuster, 1997.

Oregon Trail: Chasing the Dream illustrated by Sally Wern Comport. Simon & Schuster, 2005.

Pulling the Lion's Tail illustrated by Floyd Cooper. Simon & Schuster, 1995.

Rain Romp illustrated by Dyanna Wolcott. HarperCollins, 2002.

River Friendly, River Wild illustrated by Neil Brennan. Simon & Schuster, 2000.

Saba: Under the Hyena's Foot illustrated by Jean-Paul Tibbles. Pleasant Company Publications, 2003.

The Storyteller's Beads. Harcourt, 1998.

Terrific Connections with Authors, Illustrators and Storytellers: Real Space and Virtual Links with Toni Buzzeo. Libraries Unlimited, 1999.

35 Best Books for Teaching U.S. Regions with Toni Buzzeo. Instructor Books, 2002.

Treasury of the Southwest: Resources for Teachers and Students. Libraries Unlimited, 1992.

Trouble illustrated by Durga Bernhard. Gulliver Books, 1997.

Water Hole Waiting illustrated by Lee Christiansen. HarperCollins, 2002.

Rain Romp Script

Roles

Mom	Narrator One	Narrator Three
Dad	Narrator Two	Chorus (Four readers)

Chorus: Gray day.
Gray, grouchy day.

Narrator One: Mom tugs my toes.

Mom: Time to rise and shine!

Narrator One: I won't get up.
I don't feel shiny.

Chorus: The sky agrees with her.

Narrator Two: Dad hums a snazzy, jazzy tune.

Dad: *(Croon.)* Ohhh, it's nice to get up before nine. Or noon.

Narrator One: No way.
Nooooo way!

Chorus: The window-rattling wind agrees with her.

Narrator Two: Mom and Dad waltz up and down.

Narrator Three: Dad yodels.
Mom laughs.

Narrator One: I snarl and frown.

Chorus: Drip drop. Drip drop.
The rain agrees with her.

Mom: Mad as a wet hen.

Dad: Definitely!

Mom and Dad: I think we'd better just let her be.

Narrator One: Wet hen?
Pooh!
The sky and I are two …

Chorus:	howling prowling scowling wolverines.
Narrator One:	I leap out of bed, knock over my chairs, rush down the stairs, burst out of the house.
Chorus:	RAAAAAAIN STOMP!
Narrator Two:	Mom's and Dad's faces bob in the window like two balloons.
Narrator One:	Scolding, frowning, puzzling, smiling, laughing.
Mom and Dad:	Hey!
Chorus:	RAAAAAAIN ROMP!

Narrator One and Mom and Dad:
> We dance in whooshing, swooshing leaves.
> The thunder rumbles, shaking our bones.
> Little silver worms of rain
> wriggle and slither under our shirts.

Narrator Two:	The whole world smells like dark, wet dirt.
Narrator One:	I stretch out my hands to Dad and Mom.
Narrator Three:	The grouchiness is almost gone. And gradually the storm is, too.
Chorus:	The thunder quits grumbling. The wind fizzles. The rain drizzles, drips, and finally stops.
Narrator Two:	The wolverines have wandered off.
Narrator One:	The sky and I are soft gray moths. I think it's time to go inside. I wave the sky good-bye.
Narrator Three:	Dad builds a fire that cracks and clicks, nibbles the middles out of sticks.

Narrator One: We hold our fingers to the strands.
The warmth leaps out and licks our hands.

Narrator Three: Dad yodels.
Mom laughs.

Narrator One: I start to sing.

Narrator Two: It's time for games and giggling.

Narrator One: When I'm cold, and when I'm hot,
when I'm cheerful, when I'm not—

Narrator One and Mom and Dad:

the three of us will always be
an all-weather,
stick-together,
stomp-it-out,
romp-it-out,

All: love-you, hug-you family.

The End

Rain Romp Activities

Science Connection

Weather Words

Invite students to join you in creating a list of weather words and a list of weather phrases in *Rain Romp* using the Weather Words graphic organizer on page 88. Discuss the way these words paint a picture of the rainy day.

Then ask students to choose another type of weather, perhaps weather prevalent in your region of the country or in your current season. Begin by listing single words associated with that weather (e.g., snow, storm, flakes) and then invite students to create descriptive phrases that describe the weather (e.g., mounds of cotton, sparkling branches). Add to the graphic organizer.

Science Standards

Earth and Space Sciences

- Understands atmospheric processes and the water cycle

Social Studies Connection

Family to the Rescue

Begin by discussing the relationships between the three characters in *Rain Romp* and the students' own family configurations, honoring each family as a unique unit. Discuss the events of the story, asking students to explain how the grouchy narrator of the story was cheered up by her parents. Ask students to think of and describe a time when they were grouchy and members of their family cheered them up. What did that family member do? Ask students to think of other family members and actions that would have worked to cheer them also. Finally, ask students to think of and describe a time when they cheered up a family member. What did they do?

Behavioral Studies Standards

- Understands conflict, cooperation, and interdependence among individuals, groups, and institutions

---

Language Arts Connections

Simile and Metaphor Hunt

Jane Kurtz uses similes and metaphors to enrich her text. Begin by explaining to your students that while a simile is a comparison that uses the words "like" or "as," a metaphor is also a comparison, but without using those words. Rather, it states the comparison as fact. Invite students to go on a simile and metaphor hunt in *Rain Romp*. As students locate examples in the text, add them to your Simile and Metaphor Hunt graphic organizer on page 89.

Language Arts Standards

Reading

- Uses reading skills and strategies to understand and interpret a variety of literary texts

  - Grades 3–5: Understands the ways in which language is used in literary texts (e.g., personification, alliteration, onomatopoeia, simile, metaphor, imagery, hyperbole, beat, rhythm)

Simile and Metaphor Magic

After completing Simile and Metaphor Hunt on page 86, invite students to create their own similes and metaphors. Demonstrate the ways in which a simile can become a metaphor by removing the comparison words.

If you have completed the Weather Words activity from page 86, ask students to create weather similes and metaphors for their chosen weather before beginning the Story Building activity below.

Language Arts Standards

Writing

- Uses the stylistic and rhetorical aspects of writing

  - Grades 3–5: Uses descriptive language that clarifies and enhances ideas (e.g., common figures of speech, sensory details)

Story Building

Invite students to write a new weather story using the weather words and weather phrases they created in the Weather Words activity on page 86 as well the similes and metaphors they created in Simile and Metaphor Magic. Use *Rain Romp* as a model. For example, your first lines might read:

> Whistling winds.
>
> Wild whistling winds.
>
> Mom tugs my toes.
>
> "Rise and shine," she says.

Language Arts Standards

Writing

- Uses the stylistic and rhetorical aspects of writing

- Uses grammatical and mechanical conventions in written compositions

Rhyme Time

Rain Romp is not a rhyming story, but Jane Kurtz nevertheless often delights the reader with surprise rhyme. Invite students to locate the pairs of rhyming words at the end of lines in the story.

Language Arts Standards

Reading

- Uses reading skills and strategies to understand and interpret a variety of literary texts

  - Grades 3–5: Understands the ways in which language is used in literary texts (e.g., personification, alliteration, onomatopoeia, simile, metaphor, imagery, hyperbole, beat, rhythm)

Weather Words

Weather Words from Rain Romp	Weather Phrases from Rain Romp

Weather Words for _____	Weather Phrases for _____

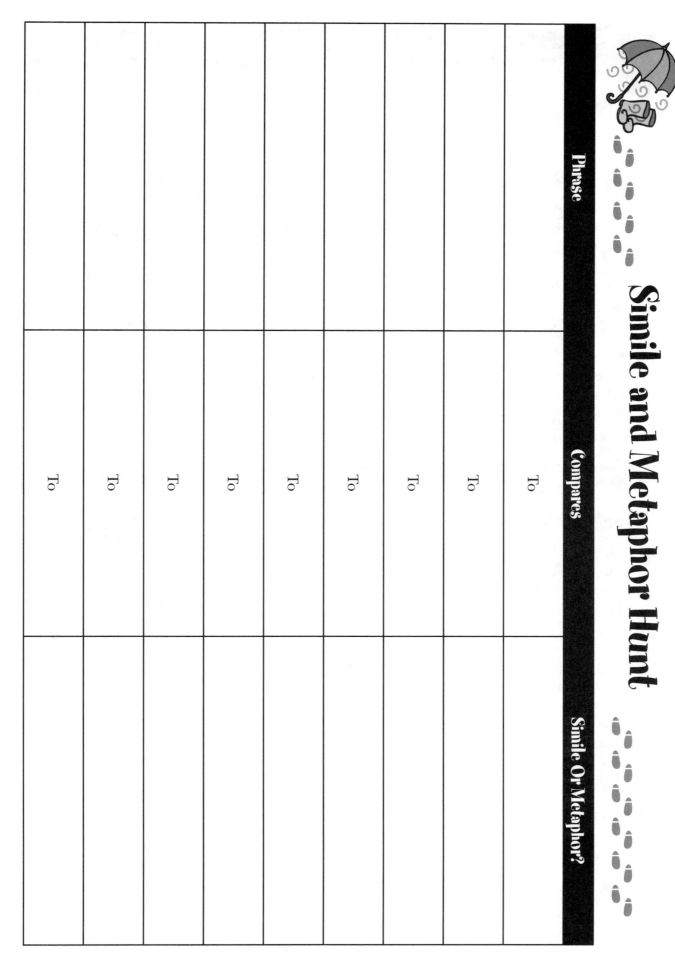

Simile and Metaphor Hunt

Phrase	Compares	Simile Or Metaphor?
	To	
	To	
	To	
	To	
	To	
	To	
	To	
	To	
	To	

The Recess Queen

Read *The Recess Queen* and the interview with Alexis O'Neill below to familiarize yourself with the book and the author. Once you are ready to perform the script with your students, read the book aloud to the children so that they can enjoy the illustrations and become familiar with the story. Then, hand out a set of photocopied scripts to ten children. Ask the remaining children to be the audience. Have performers face the audience and simply read their parts on the first run-through. Once all readers are comfortable with their parts, have a second reading with the opportunity to use props or costumes, if desired, and to act out the story while reading.

Meet Alexis O'Neill

Alexis O'Neill is the author of *Loud Emily, The Recess Queen,* and *Estela's Swap.* Her work has appeared in *Cricket, Cobblestone, Calliope, Faces, Writer's Digest,* and *The Los Angeles Times.* Alexis, a former elementary school teacher, is a Regional Advisor for the SCBWI a founder of the Children's Authors Network (CAN!), a teacher for the UCLA Extension Writer's Program, and a museum education consultant. A popular school visit presenter, Alexis weaves music, movement, and dramatic play into her assemblies as she encourages kids to "play with words!"

What was your inspiration for *The Recess Queen*? Do you have a personal connection to the story?

AO: Do you mean, have I ever been bullied? As a former elementary school teacher, I saw lots of bullies in my day. As a kid myself, I wasn't bullied. But I was bullied as an adult.

In fact, because of one impossible boss, I quit a job and became a writer. So I guess I should thank that boss for inspiring the creation of *The Recess Queen!*

Many adults assume that children's writers begin a story with a lesson in mind they want to teach their young readers. That, of course, isn't often true. But in *The Recess Queen*, a story with a strong, practical lesson, DID you have that lesson in mind when you began?

AO: A lesson in mind? Never. Kids run from preachy stories. You may think this is silly, but my story began because I liked the way that the words "mean," "Jean," and "queen" rhymed. Then I began to wonder where this mean queen might reign—and that's how I came up with the setting of the school

playground. In my first draft in 1992, I had lots of fun describing Jean's meanness, but I had no story. I began thinking, "I wonder if there's a way to get a bully to stop being a bully?" It took me until 1999 to figure out a plausible answer. Once I had the character of Katie Sue, the story fell into place.

What were you like as a child? Were you a Mean Jean, a Katie Sue, or someone else entirely?

AO: I think I've always been more of a Katie Sue. I tend to round up folks who are stragglers and make them part of a group. But my little sister, Donna, might tell you I was a "Mean Jean" when I tried to boss her around as we were growing up in Wakefield, Massachusetts.

In your book, the main character, Mean Jean, comes to solve her own problem as a result of the strong will and encouragement of Katie Sue. Did you consider other resolutions for the conflict before you settled on this solution?

AO: No. This was the only solution. I suppose that's why it took me seven years to come up with it! I took a cue from one of my nieces, an only child. As she grew up, I noticed how she played with other kids. She'd see someone standing alone and she'd say, "Hey—you want to play?" And they would. She didn't care who they were—a boy, girl, or adult. She just invited folks to play—and they did. That's when the lightbulb went off in my head. I realized that my story needed a kid who didn't care about the bully—a kid who just said, "Hey— you want to play?" and expected Jean to say, "Okay." And she did.

It's very refreshing to have a children's "problem" book where there are no adult characters. In its various drafts, did *The Recess Queen* ever have adult characters?

AO: Adults never had a role in *The Recess Queen*. I believe strongly that kids have the power to solve problems on their own.

One of the most delightful aspects of this book, for reading aloud AND for reader's theater, is your playful language. Can you tell us more about the writing process and how all this delicious language arose?

AO: In the first draft, I wrote, "She'd push 'em and smoosh 'em .... Hammer 'em, slammer 'em kitz and kajammer 'em." Don't ask me where the words came from—the words just popped out of my pen! Then, when I worked on other drafts, I took a cue from those words and pushed the language. I added the word, "lollapaloosh" to the "push and smoosh" sequence. As you know, I made up the words, "lollapaloosh" and "kitz and kajammer." But they do have a basis in two real words: "lollapalooza," which means a big exciting event, and "katzenjammer," which means a loud discordant noise. To me, they seemed to describe Mean Jean perfectly, so they became a refrain in the book.

How can readers learn more about you and your books?

AO: They can start at my Web site at www. alexisoneill.com. They can also see the online interview by Scholastic at books.scholastic.com/teachers/authors andbooks/authorstudies/authorstudies.jsp.

Books by Alexis O'Neill

Estela's Swap illustrated by Enrique O. Sanchez. Lee & Low Books, 2002.

Loud Emily illustrated by Nancy Carpenter. Simon & Schuster, 1998.

The Recess Queen illustrated by Laura Huliska-Beith. Scholastic, 2002.

The Recess Queen

Roles

Mean Jean   Narrator One   Narrator Three

Katie Sue   Narrator Two   Chorus (Four—or more—readers)

Kid One

Chorus:	Mean Jean was Recess Queen and nobody said any different.
Narrator One:	Nobody swung until Mean Jean swung.
Narrator Two:	Nobody kicked until Mean Jean kicked.
Narrator Three:	Nobody bounced until Mean Jean bounced.
Narrator One:	If kids ever crossed her, she'd …
Chorus:	push 'em and smoosh 'em, lollapaloosh 'em, hammer 'em, slammer 'em, kitz and kajammer 'em.
Mean Jean:	*(Growl.)* Say **what?**
Mean Jean:	*(Howl.)* Say **who?**
Mean Jean:	Say **you!** Just who do you think you're talking to?
Narrator One:	Mean Jean always got her way.
Narrator Two:	**Until** one day …
Narrator Three:	… a new kid came to school.
Katie Sue:	Me, Katie Sue!
Narrator One:	A teeny kid.
Narrator Two:	A tiny kid.
Narrator Three:	A kid you might scare with a jump and a …
Chorus:	**Boo!**
Narrator One:	But when the recess bell went …
Chorus:	ringity-ring,

Narrator Two:	this kid ran …
Chorus:	zingity-zing,
Narrator Three:	for the playground gate.
Narrator One:	Katie Sue **swung** before Mean Jean swung.
Narrator Two:	Katie Sue **kicked** before Mean Jean kicked.
Narrator Three:	Katie Sue **bounced** before Mean Jean bounced. The kid you might scare with a jump and a …
Chorus:	**Boo!**
Katie Sue:	Me, Katie Sue!
Narrator Three:	was too new to know about …
Chorus:	Mean Jean the Recess Queen.
Narrator One:	Well, Mean Jean bullied through the playground crowd. Like always, she …
Chorus:	pushed kids and smooshed kids, lollapalooshed kids, hammered 'em, slammered 'em, kitz and kajammered 'em
Narrator Two:	as she charged after …
Katie Sue:	Me, Katie Sue!
Mean Jean:	*(Growl.)* Say **what?**
Mean Jean:	*(Howl.)* Say **who?**
Mean Jean:	*(Snarl.)* Say **you!**
Narrator Three:	She snarled and grabbed Katie Sue by the collar.
Mean Jean:	Nobody swings until Queen Jean swings. Nobody kicks until Queen Jean kicks. Nobody bounces until Queen Jean bounces.
Narrator One:	She figured that would set the record straight.
Narrator Two:	She figured wrong.
Narrator Three:	Katie Sue talked back! Just as sassy as could be.
Katie Sue:	How **did** you get so bossy?
Narrator One:	Then that puny thing, that loony thing,
Narrator Two:	grabbed the ball and bounced away.

Narrator Three:	Oh! Katie Sue was one quick kid. She bolted quick as lightning.
Chorus:	Bouncity bouncity **bounce.** Kickity kickity **kick.** Swingity swingity **swing.**
Narrator One:	Mean Jean thundered close behind.
Chorus:	**Bouncity, kickity, swingity.**
Narrator Two:	The Recess Queen was **not** amused.
Narrator Three:	She raced and chased and in-your-faced …
Katie Sue:	Me, Katie Sue!
Narrator One:	No one spoke.
Narrator Two:	No one moved.
Narrator Three:	No one **breathed.**
Narrator One:	Then from her pack pulled Katie Sue a jump rope clean and bright.
Katie Sue:	*(Sing.)* Hey, Jeanie Beanie, let's try this jump rope out!
Narrator Two:	Here's one thing true—until that day, no one **dared** ask Mean Jean to play.
Narrator Three:	But that Katie Sue just hopped and jumped and skipped away.
Katie Sue:	I like ice cream, I like tea, I want Jean to jump with me!
Narrator One:	Jean just gaped and stared as if too **scared** to move at all.
Narrator Two:	So Katie Sue sang once more.
Katie Sue:	I like popcorn, I like tea, I want Jean to jump with me!
Narrator Three:	Then from the side a kid called out,
Kid One:	**Go, Jean, go!**
Narrator Three:	And too surprised to even shout, Jean jumped in with Katie Sue.
Mean Jean and Katie Sue:	
	I like cookies, I like tea, I want **you** to jump with me!
Narrator One:	The rope whizzed and slapped,
Chorus:	**faster, faster,**

Narrator Two:	the rope spun and flapped,
Chorus:	**faster, faster!**
Narrator Three:	Till it caught in a tangled disaster. But they just giggled and …
Chorus:	**jumped again!**
Narrator One:	**Well**—now when recess rolls around that playground's one great place.
Narrator Two:	At the school bell's …
Chorus:	ringity-ring,
Narrator Two:	those two girls race …
Chorus:	zingity-zing,
Narrator Two:	out the classroom door.
Narrator Three:	Jean doesn't …
Chorus:	push kids and smoosh kids, lollapaloosh kids, hammer 'em, slammer 'em, kitz and kajammer 'em—
Narrator Three:	'cause she's having too much fun—
Chorus:	rompity-romping,
Narrator Three:	with her **friends.**
Chorus:	Bouncity, kickity, swingity, hoppity, skippity, jumpity, ringity, zingity,
All:	**Yesssss!**

❧

The End

The Recess Queen Activities

Language Arts Connections

Text to Text Connections

After reading *The Recess Queen*, read *Bootsie Barker Bites* by Barbara Bottner (Putnam, 1992) aloud to the class and invite comparison and discussion. Use the Text to Text Connections Venn diagram on page 99 to facilitate discussion.

- How does Jean bully?

- How does Bootsie bully?

- What would Jean do in *Bootsie Barker Bites*? What would Katie Sue do?

- What would Bootsie do in *The Recess Queen*? What would the *Bootsie Barker Bites* narrator do?

Language Arts Standards

Reading

- Uses reading skills and strategies to understand and interpret a variety of literary texts

From the Diary of a Bully

As a class, discuss the possible reasons for Jean bullying her classmates. Ask students to decide whether she is simply a mean person or whether things in her life might cause her to behave as she does. After this discussion, invite students to write a series of journal entries from Mean Jean's perspective.

Language Arts Standards

Writing

- Uses the stylistic and rhetorical aspects of writing

A "Bully" is a Noun, "To Bully" is a Verb

Review the functions of nouns and verbs with students. Then discuss words that are used as both nouns and verbs such as "boss," "nurse," "coach," and "cook." Explain that "bully" is also such a word. Mean Jean is a bully but she also "bullies" her classmates.

Begin by looking up definitions of the noun and verb forms of "bully" in a children's dictionary. Now, focus students' attention on the verbal form of the word. Although Alexis O'Neill never uses the verb "bully" in *The Recess Queen*, she shows us that Jean is a bully through her use of other verbs. Ask students to think about other verbs in the story, such as "push" and "smoosh," that show the reader that Jean is bullying. As a class use chart paper (or, if you have multiple copies of the book, in small groups) use the A "Bully" Is a Noun, "To Bully" Is a Verb graphic organizer on page 100 to list the bullying verbs O'Neill employs.

Language Arts Standards

Reading

- Uses reading skills and strategies to understand and interpret a variety of literary texts

Jump Rope Rhymes

Jump rope rhymes are rhythmic, creative poetry just right for jumping rope. One of the special things about Katie Sue is that she solves the bullying problem with Jean by using jump rope rhymes she makes up herself.

Read selections from *Over in the Pink House: New Jump Rope Rhymes* by Rebecca Kai Dotlich (Boyds Mills Press, 2004) and *Anna Banana: 101 Jump Rope Rhymes* by Joanna Cole (HarperTrophy, 1989) and invite students to chant their favorites along with you. Then ask students to create jump rope rhymes of their own. Compile a class book and host a recess jumpathon!

Language Arts Standards

Writing

- Uses the stylistic and rhetorical aspects of writing

Listening and Speaking

- Uses listening and speaking strategies for different purposes

Physical Education Standards

- Uses a variety of basic and advanced movement forms

- Uses movement concepts and principles in the development of motor skills

Social Studies Connections

Cooperation and Respect

Begin this activity in the library media center by locating the definitions for the two words "cooperation" and "respect" in as many different dictionaries as are available at your students' reading levels. Record definitions on a series of large sheets of chart paper and display them around the room. Next, read all of the definitions for each word aloud to the group and combine and rephrase to create class definitions of the two words.

Once you have class definitions, invite students to use the Cooperation and Respect graphic organizer on page 101. Brainstorm a list of examples of Mean Jean's uncooperative and disrespectful behaviors on the right side and a list of cooperative and respectful behaviors they might engage in at recess on the left side. Lively discussion will ensue!

Behavioral Studies Standards

- Understands conflict, cooperation, and interdependence among individuals, groups, and institutions

Anti-Bullying

After you have completed the A "Bully" Is a Noun, "To Bully" Is a Verb graphic organizer on page 100, invite students to create a list of anti-bullying rules. Remind them that it is sometimes not enough to just say, "No bullying." Sometimes the rules need to be stated positively. For instance, "No pushing, no smooshing" might become "Only touch a classmate in a gentle and respectful way." Ask students to illustrate the rules and then post them.

Behavioral Studies Standards

- Understands conflict, cooperation, and interdependence among individuals, groups, and institutions

Handling a Bully

Sometimes the only way to handle a bully at school is to ask for help from a teacher or other adult. But sometimes, as in *The Recess Queen*, a wise kid like Katie Sue can figure out a solution himself or herself. Ask students what technique Katie Sue used to stop Jean from bullying. Why do they think it worked? If students have already completed the From the Diary of a Bully activity on page 96, discuss what they feel makes Jean behave as she does. This may help them understand why Katie Sue's approach works.

Behavioral Studies Standards

- Understands conflict, cooperation, and interdependence among individuals, groups, and institutions

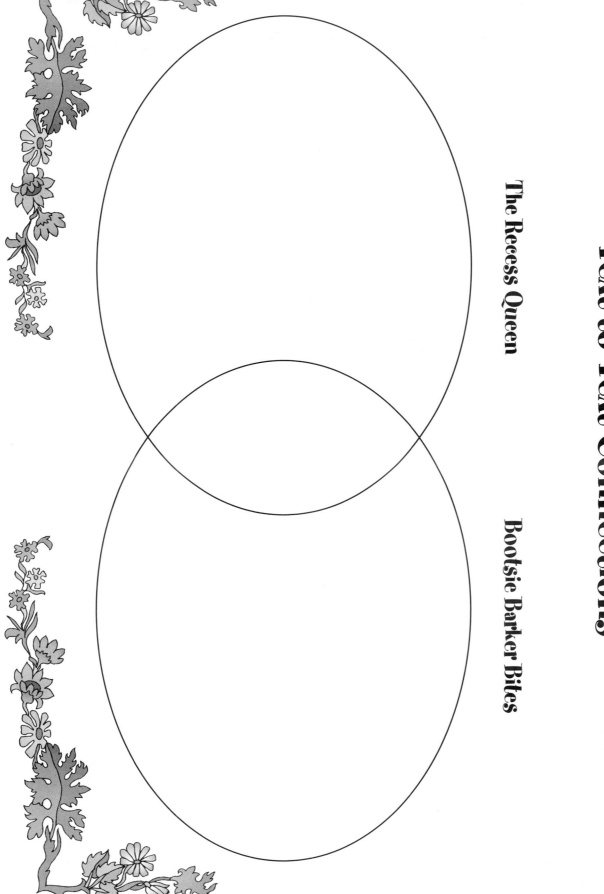

Text to Text Connections

The Recess Queen

Bootsie Barker Bites

A "Bully" Is a Noun, "To Bully" Is a Verb

VERB: to bully	
Dictionary Definition of "Bully"	Other Bullying Verbs

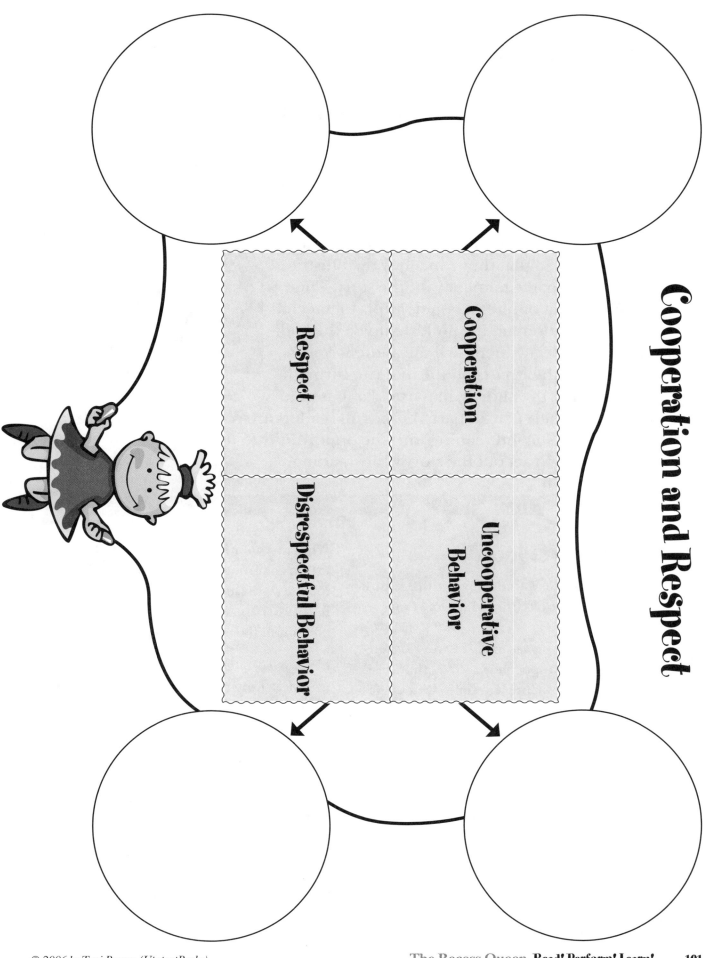

Cooperation and Respect

| Cooperation | Respect |
| Uncooperative Behavior | Disrespectful Behavior |

School Picture Day

Read *School Picture Day* and the interview with Lynn Plourde below to familiarize yourself with the book. Once you are ready to perform the script with your students, read the book aloud to the children so that they can enjoy the illustrations and become familiar with the story. Then, hand out a set of photocopied scripts to ten children. Ask the remaining children to be the audience. Have performers face the audience and simply read their parts on the first run-through. (Be sure that the chorus, in particular, has time to practice their playful parts!) Once all readers are comfortable with their parts, have a second reading with the opportunity to use props or costumes, if desired, and to act out the story while reading.

Meet Lynn Plourde

Lynn Plourde, a Maine native, is the author of 15 picture books, including *Pigs in the Mud in the Middle of the Rud, Wild Child, The First Feud,* and *Mother, May I?* Lynn worked for 20 years as a speech-language therapist and began her writing career in that profession by writing instructional books, including the Classroom Listening and Speaking series. Lynn typically does a hundred author visits a year to schools, libraries, and conferences. She prides herself on being a "teaching" author—helping students and teachers learn how to plan, write, and revise different kinds of stories.

What was your inspiration for *School Picture Day*? Do you have a personal connection to the story?

LP: *School Picture Day* was a long time coming. It took me 12 years to write that story. I have a two-inch thick folder filled with many variations. But the first version was actually called "Say Cheese, Please" about a family going for a family photo at a photographer's studio. Everyone in the family said "cheese" and was very cooperative except for one mischievous brother in the family. The idea arose after my own

family went for a photo shoot despite our two-year-old daughter's illness. In order to meet the deadline for Christmas gift giving, we kept the appointment, and our daughter "made it" through—although she wasn't very smiley. But who could blame her?

I know that *School Picture Day* is part of a series of school-related picture books you'll be publishing. Were you a teacher? If so, what role did that play in your creation of this series? Please tell us more about the other titles, too.

LP: Yes, *School Picture Day* was the first in a series of stories about Mrs. Shepherd's class. I had so much fun with it, I wanted to write another. My editor suggested I write a story featuring a different student in Mrs. Shepherd's class as the main character. Since then, I've written *Teacher Appreciation Day* about Maybella Jean Wishywashy who can't decide how to show her appreciation to Mrs. Shepherd, *Pajama Day* about Drew A. Blank who forgets everything he needs to celebrate Pajama Day at school, and *Book Fair Day* about a boy named Dewey Booker who will try anything to visit the book fair early. (A fun little secret in the books is that each of the characters from earlier books are true to character in the new books—and so Josephina is still fiddling in the later books; the story doesn't say so, but the illustrations show that it's so.)

I worked as a speech-language therapist in elementary schools for more than 20 years—so I was very familiar with schools and kids and all the silly possibilities for classroom stories. The teacher in this series is named Mrs. Shepherd for a couple of reasons. I liked the idea of "shepherd" since a teacher leads a flock of students.

Also, my second grade teacher was named Mrs. Shepherd when I went to a two-room schoolhouse in Skowhegan, Maine, back in the 1960s (my class photo with the real Mrs. Shepherd is on my Web site).

Many readers will feel, as I do, a strong attraction to Josephina Caroleena Wattasheena the First. She's such a strong and independent character, following her own inner voice and passion. Were you like Josephina as a child?

LP: Actually, no. I was more of a quiet, apple-polishing kid in school. Always wanting to please the teachers, I worked very hard at following all the rules and doing everything they asked plus a little more. I think I'm jealous of Josephina—I wished I had been more independent when I was younger. But one of my kids was like her. My youngest stepson Seth used to fiddle and fidget with everything, taking things apart to see how they worked. Once, he dumped a whole bottle of dish detergent down the sink to see how to make bubbles, and when we told him he couldn't do that again, the very next day he made bubbles with a whole bottle of shampoo instead!

In your book, Josephina's character flaw both causes the havoc in the classroom and also leads to the solution of the problem. Did you consider other resolutions for the story? Will you tell us more about how this plot structure developed?

LP: I did not consider any other endings. I knew from the beginning that Josephina's character flaw would have to save the day in the story—and it did! And all the other stories in the series follow the same plan or plot structure which is very simple: a

character with a flaw (e.g., lazy, clumsy) is in a situation (e.g., birthday party, camping trip) and that character's flaw gets in the way, gets in the way, gets in the way, and finally saves the day. It's a fun kind of story to write, and I've enjoyed teaching many students how to write their own "character" stories. A word of caution though—students need to learn the structure of stories as readers first, and after that as writers.

The photographer's character is so much fun in *School Picture Day*! He's so refreshingly childlike. What (or who) was your inspiration for him?

LP: I didn't have one particular person in mind, but rather photographers as a group. I think it's so funny to watch photographers in schools or stores. They will do anything to make their subjects laugh—including making fools of themselves. I just tried to exaggerate that quality in the photographer in *School Picture Day*.

Your book is full of delightfully playful language. Can you tell us more about your word choices—and creations—for this book?

LP: I'm not sure if it's the speech-language therapist in me (who had to be aware of all the sounds in the English language) or the reader in me (who has always stopped to savor and reread words that are pleasing to the ear) or the author in me (who began to play with alliteration and onomatopoeia), or maybe a combination of all of them, but I do delight in words and the sounds of words. In fact I call myself a "word player" rather than an author. I combine words in fun ways. I make up words. And the result is words like "highfalutin fidgeting, fiddling,

fuddling, and foopling" that are just plain fun to hear and say. I call words like that "ear candy."

One more thing—Thor Wickstrom, the illustrator of the Mrs. Shepherd series, obviously enjoys playing with words, too. The words that the "windup, flashing, squawking, talking bird" says in *School Picture Day* were written by Thor Wickstrom, the illustrator—not me, the author! And I was delighted he added them.

How can readers learn more about you and your books?

LP: First of all by reading my books—I think books reveal so much about their authors. Plus by visiting my Web site at www.lynnplourde.com, which has lots of background on my books, information on me as a kid and my family, writing advice, plus lots of learning activities for my books.

Books by Lynn Plourde

Book Fair Day illustrated by Thor Wickstrom. Dutton, 2006.

A Celebration of Maine Children's Books with Paul Knowles. University of Maine Press, 1998.

Classroom Listening and Speaking series. Communication Skills Institute.

Dad, Aren't You Glad? illustrated by Amy Wummer. Penguin, 2005.

The First Feud between the Mountain and the Sea illustrated by Jim Sollers. Down East Books, 2003.

Grandpappy Snippy Snappies illustrated by Christopher Santoro. HarperCollins, 2002.

Moose, of Course! illustrated by Jim Sollers. Down East Books, 1999.

Mother, May I? illustrated by Amy Wummer. Penguin, 2004.

Pajama Day illustrated by Thor Wickstrom. Penguin, 2005.

Pigs in the Mud in the Middle of the Rud illustrated by John Schoenherr. Scholastic, 1997.

School Picture Day illustrated by Thor Wickstrom. Penguin, 2002.

Science Fair Day illustrated by Thor Wickstrom. Dutton, 2007.

Snow Day illustrated by Hideko Takahashi. Simon & Schuster, 2001.

Spring's Sprung illustrated by Greg Couch. Simon & Schuster, 2002.

Summer's Vacation illustrated by Greg Couch. Simon & Schuster, 2003.

Teacher Appreciation Day illustrated by Thor Wickstrom. Penguin, 2003.

Thank You, Grandpa illustrated by Jason Cockcroft. Penguin, 2003.

Wild Child illustrated by Greg Couch. Simon & Schuster, 1999.

Winter Waits illustrated by Greg Couch. Simon & Schuster, 2001.

School Picture Day Script

Roles	
Josephina	Birdie
Mrs. Shepherd	Narrator One
Photographer	Narrator Two
	Narrator Three
	Chorus (Three readers)

Narrator One:	It was school picture day.
Narrator Two:	Everyone was dressed in their best—
Chorus:	bows and bow ties, sashes and suspenders, jewels and jackets.
Narrator Three:	Everyone, that is, except …
Josephina:	Me! Josephina Caroleena Wattasheena the First.
Narrator One:	Josephina didn't know it was school picture day.
Narrator Two:	She didn't even know it was Wednesday.
Narrator Three:	She had more important things to think about on the bus ride to school.
Josephina:	Hmmm. I wonder how this gearshift works.
Chorus:	SQUIRM SHIFT SQUEAL LIFT
Narrator One:	After some …
Chorus:	highfalutin' fidgeting, fiddling, fuddling, and foopling …
Narrator One:	Josephina finally figured out how the gearshift worked.
Chorus:	SPLOOCH!
Narrator Two:	Meanwhile, everyone wiped the grease off their …
Chorus:	bows and bow ties, sashes and suspenders, jewels and jackets,
Narrator Three:	as they walked the last three-and-a-half miles to school.

Mrs. Shepherd:	Hustle, bustle, hurry, scurry.
Narrator One:	Mrs. Shepherd rushed everyone into her classroom.
Mrs. Shepherd:	You're late, and the photographer will be here any minute to take our class picture. Now please, everyone, fill out the school picture form with your sharpest number-2 pencils.
Narrator Two:	Mrs. Shepherd glanced toward Josephina and added ...
Mrs. Shepherd:	and no fiddling.
Narrator Three:	Everyone started filling out the forms, after sharpening their pencils at Mrs. Shepherd's super-fast, plush-deluxe electric pencil sharpener. Everyone, that is, except ...
Josephina:	Me! Josephina Caroleena Wattasheena the First.
Narrator Three:	She had more important things to think about.
Chorus:	WIGGLE YANK JIGGLE CRANK!
Josephina:	Hmmm. I wonder how this pencil sharpener works.
Narrator One:	After some ...
Chorus:	highfalutin' fidgeting, fiddling, fuddling, and foopling ...
Narrator One:	Josephina finally figured out how the pencil sharpener worked.
Narrator Two:	Meanwhile, everyone brushed wood shavings off their ...
Chorus:	bows and bow ties, sashes and suspenders, jewels and jackets, and bun.
Narrator Three:	They finished their brushing just in time.
Mrs. Shepherd:	Here's the photographer.
Photographer:	Time to line up, you cutesie wootsies.
Narrator One:	The photographer scurried Mrs. Shepherd and all twenty-three children in the class into their places:
Chorus:	the stand-on-the-chairs row, the stand-on-the-floor row, the sit-on-the-chairs row, and the sit-on-the-floor row.
Josephina:	He put me in the stand-on-the-chairs row.

Photographer:	Everyone, say cheesy wheezy, if you pleasy.
Chorus and Mrs. Shepherd:	
	Cheesy wheezy.
Narrator Three:	But Josephina had more important things to think about. She lifted up a ceiling tile and muttered.
Josephina:	Hmmm. I wonder how this sprinkler system works.
Chorus:	PUSH SHOVE PWOOSH ABOVE!
Narrator One:	After some …
Chorus:	highfalutin' fidgeting, fiddling, fuddling, and foopling …
Narrator One:	Josephina finally figured out how the sprinkler system worked.
Narrator Two:	Meanwhile, twenty-two children, Mrs. Shepherd, and the photographer wrung out their …
Chorus:	bows and bow ties, sashes and suspenders, jewels and jackets, bun and camera.
Photographer:	Okey dokey. Don't be a slow pokey.
Narrator One:	The photographer lined everyone up in their same exact places.
Josephina:	*Except* me, Josephina. He put me in the sit-on-the-floor row.
Photographer:	*(Coax.)* Teethy weethies. Let's see those teethies.
Narrator Two:	Twenty-two children and Mrs. Shepherd showed their teethies.
Narrator Three:	But Josephina had more important things to think about.
Chorus:	PRY CREAK RATTLE PEEK!
Narrator Three:	Josephina lifted up a floor vent and muttered.
Josephina:	Hmmm. I wonder how this heating system works.
Narrator One:	After some …
Chorus:	highfalutin' fidgeting, fiddling, fuddling, and foopling …
Narrator One:	Josephina finally figured out how the heating system worked.

Narrator Two: Meanwhile, twenty-two children, Mrs. Shepherd, and the photographer stomped the soot off their ...

Chorus: bows and bow ties,
sashes and suspenders,
jewels and jackets,
bun and camera.

Photographer: One more time, you sweetie pies. Just watch my little birdie.

Narrator One: The photographer got out his special windup, flashing, squawking, talking bird and lined everyone up, back in their same exact places.

Josephina: *Except* me, Josephina. He put me in the sit-on-the-chairs row.

Photographer: *(Beg.)* Birdie wants a cheesy cheesy. Me-sy wants a cheesy cheesy too.

Chorus and Mrs. Shepherd:
Cheesy cheesy, cheesy cheesy.

Narrator Two: Everyone said cheesy, *except* the bird ...

Birdie: SQUAWK! HOWDY! WAZZUP?

Narrator Three: And *except* Josephina. She had more important things to think about. She sat in her chair muttering.

Josephina: Hmmm. I wonder what makes this special windup, flashing, squawking, talking bird work.

Birdie: SQUAWK! YO! ME FRIEND!

Narrator One: After some ...

Chorus: highfalutin' fidgeting, fiddling, fuddling, and foopling ...

Narrator One: Josephina finally figured out how the special windup, flashing, squawking, talking bird worked.

Birdie: SQUAWK! SQUAWK! SPROINK!

Chorus: FLUFF POOF CRANK KERZOOF!

Narrator Two: Meanwhile, twenty-two children, Mrs. Shepherd, and the photographer plucked feathers off their ...

Chorus: bows and bow ties,
sashes and suspenders,
jewels and jackets,
bun and camera.

Photographer:	*(Yell.)* FREEZE! I SAID, FREEZE!
Narrator Three:	The photographer yelled so loud everyone could see his toe bones.
Narrator Two:	This time Mrs. Shepherd and twenty-*three* children froze.
Narrator Three:	No cheesies. No teethies. But they were *all* looking at the camera.
Narrator One:	The photographer hurried to push the button.
Chorus:	Kl-i-i-i-i- i-i-i-i-c- r- o-o-o- o- o-
Photographer:	*(Scream.)* Aah! My camera doesn't work!
Chorus:	Then fix it.
Photographer:	I don't know how to fix it. I don't know how it works. All I do is push the button.
Mrs. Shepherd:	*(Gasp.)* You can't fix it?
Chorus:	*(Sob.)* We won't have our school pictures taken?
Photographer:	No-sy wo-sy.
Narrator Two:	The photographer shook his head.
Chorus:	SHIMMY TWEEZLE PUTTER QUEEZLE!
Narrator Three:	Josephina held the camera muttering.
Josephina:	Hmmm. I wonder how this camera works.
Narrator One:	After some ...
Chorus:	highfalutin' fidgeting, fiddling, fuddling, and foopling . . .
Narrator One:	Josephina finally figured out how the camera worked.
Josephina:	It works.
Mrs. Shepherd:	Nice fiddling.
Photographer:	*(Begs.)* Sweetie, munchkin, pumpkin pie. Show me! Show me!
Josephina:	Okay. Everyone, line up, back in your same exact places, *except* you.

Narrator Two:	She put the photographer in the lie-on-the-floor row.
Narrator Three:	Then she pushed the time-delay button on the camera, ran to her place, and simply said ...
Josephina:	Smile.
Narrator Two:	Twenty-three children, Mrs. Shepherd, and the photographer all smiled.
Narrator One:	Several weeks later, the school pictures arrived.
Mrs. Shepherd:	Josephina, please hand these out.
Narrator Three:	Josephina had more important things to think about—like her new spaceship science project—but she passed them out anyway.
Narrator One:	Everyone was pretty pleased. But all the parents did wonder:
Narrator Two:	Who was that new big kid in Mrs. Shepherd's class?
Photographer:	Cheesy wheezy!

The End

School Picture Day Activities

Social Studies Connection

What Kind of Smart Is Josephina?

Review the Multiple Intelligences and the What Kind of Smart are You? activities in the *Violet's Music* section (page 123) and be sure that students are familiar with the nine intelligences before beginning. As they did with Violet in *Violet's Music,* ask them to discuss Josephina's predominant intelligence in *School Picture Day.* Once they have identified her primary intelligence, ask them where in the story they got their first clue about it. Then ask them to supply specific evidence that she exhibited that intelligence throughout the story as they fill out the What Kind of Smart Is Josephina? graphic organizer on page 115.

Behavioral Studies Standards

- Understands that interactions among learning, inheritance, and physical development affect human behavior

Life Skills Standards

Thinking and Reasoning

- Understands and applies the basic principles of presenting an argument

Science Connections

The Right Tool for the Right Job

The very first time we see Josephina as she runs to the bus on *School Picture Day,* she is carrying her red toolbox. Josephina is always prepared! As the story unfolds, we learn more about the contents of her toolbox. Ask students to examine the illustrations carefully in each of these four instances and determine which tools Josephina has in her toolbox or is using for the task. List the tools and discuss what use Josephina might make of each tool for the task at hand.

- Job 1 (Tinkering with the gear shift on bus)

- Job 2 (Fixing the pencil sharpener)

  Job 3 (Fixing the sprinkler system)

- Job 4 (Fixing the heating system)

- Job 5 (Fixing the camera)

Helpful online resources can be found at the Enchanted Learning Web site at <u>www. enchantedlearning.com/themes/tools. shtml</u>.

You might also want to visit the Tool Gopher site (<u>www.toolgopher.com</u>) and click on Hand Tools for photographs of actual tools grouped by type to help students identify Josephina's tools.

Science Standards

Physical Sciences

- Understands forces and motion

Josephina's New and Improved Toolbox

Once students have completed The Right Tool for the Right Job activity above, invite them to imagine other situations Josephina might get herself into at school where her toolbox would come in handy. What might she want to tinker with or fix? What tools would she need for these jobs?

Consider that as Josephina becomes more skilled at fixing things, she might even want to use power tools. Return to the Tool Gopher site (www.toolgopher.com) and click on Power & Air Tools this time.

Science Standards

Physical Sciences

* Understands forces and motion

Language Arts Connections

Dressing Up

One of the pleasures of reading books by Lynn Plourde is her attention to language. As a former speech teacher, she loves words and playing with words. In fact, on her Web site and in her interview, she says that she should be called a "word player" rather than an author! When school picture day rolls around, the students in Mrs. Shepherd's class (all except for Josephina) get dressed up to have their picture taken. They wear:

> bows and bow ties
>
> sashes and suspenders
>
> jewels and jackets

Ask students to notice two things about this list. First, each pair of clothing items is alliterative. Second, each pair includes one predominantly female clothing item paired with one predominantly male clothing item.

Challenge your students to come up with additional pairings that follow the same alliterative and female/male pattern for school picture day. What else might the kids be wearing? Fill those items in on the Dressing Up graphic organizer on page 116. Then, invite your students to choose another activity, whether something that happens at school or an entirely different type of activity (sports or entertainment, perhaps) and create paired clothing or accessories for that activity on the graphic organizer.

Language Arts Standards

Writing

* Uses the stylistic and rhetorical aspects of writing

Reading

* Uses reading skills and strategies to understand and interpret a variety of literary texts

---

What Day Is It?

Author Lynn Plourde was a longtime teacher, so she knows all about special days at school. Thus far, in the Mrs. Shepherd series, she has published:

* *School Picture Day* (Dutton, 2002)
* *Teacher Appreciation Day* (Dutton, 2003)
* *Pajama Day* (Dutton, 2005)
* *Book Fair Day* (Dutton, 2006)
* *Science Fair Day* (Dutton, 2007)

Each book features a different student from Mrs. Shepherd's class and revolves around the special school day. Begin this activity by sharing these titles with the students and asking them to watch as similar patterns evolve in the stories.

Then invite students to brainstorm the special days celebrated at your school, in addition to the ones that Lynn Plourde has already written about. Create a list of these special days. As a class, choose one of these days to write a Mrs. Shepherd story.

Discuss who the main character of the story will be. What will be his or her defining characteristic and primary intelligence (if you have not already completed it, refer to the What Kind of Smart Is Josephina? activity on page 112 for more information on multiple intelligences).

Once the main character takes form for the students, decide on the problem and the ultimate solution to the problem. Following Lynn Plourde's "pattern of three" example in *School Picture Day,* how will the main character try-and-fail, try-and-fail, try-and-fail, then try-and-succeed?

Once you have done the necessary advance planning, write a new Mrs. Shepherd story celebrating a special day at your school.

Language Arts Standards

Writing

• Uses the stylistic and rhetorical aspects of writing

Reading

• Uses reading skills and strategies to understand and interpret a variety of literary texts

Art Connection

Class Picture Day

After completing the What Kind of Smart Is Josephina? activity on page 112 and the What Kind of Smart Are You? activity on page 123 for *Violet's Music,* ask students to come to school wearing or carrying at least one item that reveals their primary or secondary intelligence. Using a digital or disposable camera, allow students, one at a time, to be the class photographer, arranging the class (with their identifying articles of clothing or objects) for a class picture as the photographer did in *School Picture Day.* Ask each "photographer" to think about what organizing principles he/she will use when arranging members of the class. Create a class photo album or Multiple Intelligences display of the pictures.

Arts Standards

Visual Arts

• Knows how to use structures (e.g., sensory qualities, organizational principles, expressive features) and functions of art

What Kind of Smart Is Josephina?

PICTURE SMART: Does Josephina love to draw, design, or create beautiful things using photography or building materials?

WORD SMART: Does Josephina love words, reading, writing, telling stories, speaking, and wordplay?

NUMBER/REASONING SMART: Does Josephina love numbers, science, computers, and figuring out how things work?

BODY SMART: Does Josephina love to run or dance or play physical games and work hard?

MUSIC SMART: Does Josephina love to sing or play an instrument and love music more than anything else?

SELF SMART: Does Josephina seem to know herself especially well and is she peaceful and confident?

PEOPLE SMART: Is Josephina very good at working with others, organizing groups, and understanding other peoples' ideas?

NATURE SMART: Does Josephina love animals, being out in nature, or taking care of the environment?

WONDERING SMART: Does Josephina love to ask—and answer—BIG questions like "Why are we here on Earth?"

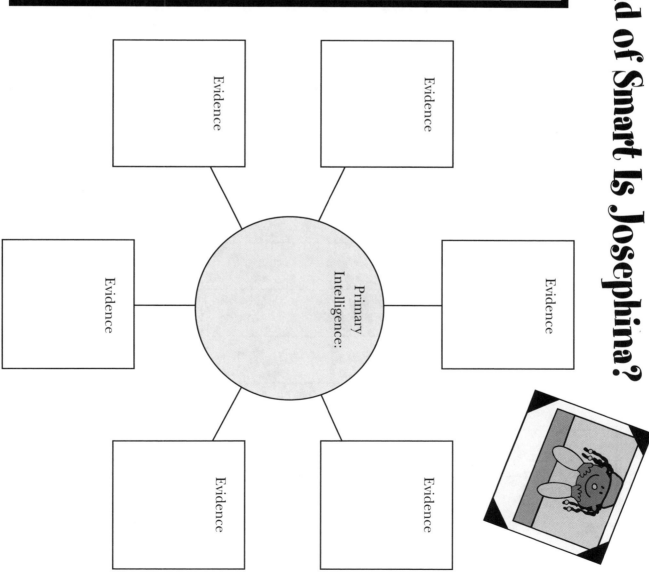

Evidence

Evidence

Evidence

Evidence

Evidence

Evidence

Primary Intelligence:

 # Dressing Up

Dressing Up for School Picture Day		
Letter	**Female Clothing**	**Male Clothing**
B	bows	bow ties
S	sashes	suspenders
J	jewels	jackets

Dressing up for _____

Letter	Female Clothing	Male Clothing

Violet's Music

Read *Violet's Music* and the interview with Angela Johnson below to familiarize yourself with the book and the author. When you are ready to perform the script with your students, read the book aloud to the children so that they can enjoy the illustrations and become familiar with the story. Then, hand out a set of photocopied scripts to ten children. Ask the remaining children to be the audience. Have performers face the audience and simply read their parts on the first run-through. Once all readers are comfortable with their parts, have a second reading with the opportunity to use props or costumes, if desired, and to act out the story while reading.

Meet Angela Johnson

Angela Johnson was born in Tuskegee, Alabama, in 1961. She is one of three children and became a writer so she could dress her younger brothers up and put them in plays. Ms. Johnson's first book was published in 1989. She has subsequently written approximately 40 books. She lives in Ohio, in an old creaky house surrounded by a beautiful garden. Ms. Johnson has been given some prestigious award recognitions including a PEN/Norma Klein Award and two Alabama Author Awards. Angela believes the only thing better than writing is sitting on her front porch thinking about writing.

***Violet's Music* is a story about a born musician. Violet exhibited her passion before she could even talk. What's your personal connection to Violet and her creative path?**

AJ: Actually, I was given so many chances as a child to be Violet. My mother smiled so expectantly when she asked me what instrument I wanted to play in fifth grade. "Nothing," said I. I still don't understand my hesitation to play an instrument. Regret is with me as I'm now an adult without any musical talent whatsoever. My parents would say I was a kiddie gadfly; but I just think the dedication was missing or I was too busy reading comic books.

The jazz influences are strong in the text of *Violet's Music*. Are you a music lover? Did you listen to any particular pieces or kinds of music as you wrote this book?

AJ: I love all kinds of music. I am a big fan of jazz. Anything Billie Holiday or Nina Simone sang knocks me out. I grew up on Motown and Rock. But I think the music I love most as an adult is Reggae. Bob Marley, Bunny Wailer ... amazing. I must say though that I'm a big fan of Baroque music also. It's perfect on Sunday mornings. But interestingly enough I don't remember listening to any music while I was writing *Violet's Music.* I normally do listen to music as I write. Maybe I just had it in my head that day.

***Violet's Music* reflects, in part, the long African-American oral tradition of "call and response," which, of course, is also a tradition in jazz music. Did you purposely set out to incorporate call and response or was it serendipity?**

AJ: I always believe that everything I write is serendipitous. It is only when the work is done that I sit back and view it at all. I'm always surprised at the end results.

My early poetry training was learned through much call and response, now that I think of it. There is an ongoing rhythm of *Violet's Music* that makes me feel comfortable (as I felt when I was learning poems to recite when I was a little girl). My first brush with poetry, it seems, was on my grandfather's knee as he recited something from Langston Hughes and I repeated it. As most children love the interactive nature of call and response, I'd guess a book about a child seeking music and others who played it would be perfect together.

I wanted Violet to take everyone on an odyssey of discovery. Everyone had to know how important music was to her at the very beginning. Also I wanted the quest for musical friends to be as wonderful as the eventual discovery of her soul mates. I hope that it was.

Many children's books have a strong message, as *Violet's Music* does. Did you set out to write a story about individualism and the value of holding fast to a dream or did it arise more organically from the character you created in Violet?

AJ: Writing does happen for me organically. I believe that Violet, in the end, told her own story. I do remember wanting to write about a character who sang. But Violet began to do oh-so-much more on her own, it seems. In the end I guess I only do the typing if the character is that strong.

There is such enormous variety in your books, from picture books to very sophisticated young adult novels like *The First Part Last*, winner of the 2004 Michael L. Printz Award for excellence in young adult literature. Even among your published picture books, there is a good deal of diversity. Please talk about what calls to you as a picture book story.

AJ: My picture books, indeed, run the gamut. My first picture books, *Tell Me a Story, Mama, The Leaving Morning,* and *When I Am Old with You,* are what I call "sweet family books." They were valentines to warm and loving relatives. They spoke to me because I was a nanny at the time and surrounded by small children and their families.

Later books like *I Dream of Trains* and *Just Like Josh Gibson* moved me along to my and my editor Kevin Lewis's love of heroes.

In between I dabbled in humor and animals—*Julius* and *The Girl Who Wore Snakes.* So I guess in the end diversity is my spice of life, and I never know what I'll be writing next.

How can readers learn more about you and your books?

AJ: I'd love for everyone to come to my house for pizza, but since this would prob-

ably be impossible because of the limited parking in my neighborhood, anyone can just go to www.visitingauthors.com to check me out when I had big hair.

Books by Angela Johnson

Aunt in Our House illustrated by David Soman. Orchard Books, 1996.

Bird. Dial, 2004.

A Cool Moonlight illustrated by Kamil Vojnar. Dial, 2003.

Daddy Calls Me Man illustrated by Rhonda Mitchell. Orchard Books, 2000.

Do Like Kyla illustrated by James E. Ransome. Orchard Books, 1990.

Down the Winding Road illustrated by Shane Evans. DK Publishing, 2000.

The First Part Last. Simon & Schuster, 2003.

The Girl Who Wore Snakes illustrated by James E. Ransome. Scholastic, 1993.

Gone from Home: Short Takes. DK Publishing, 1998.

Heaven. Simon & Schuster, 1998.

Humming Whispers. Scholastic, 1995.

I Dream of Trains illustrated by Mike Benny and Loren Long. Simon & Schuster, 2003.

Joshua by the Sea illustrated by Rhonda Mitchell. Scholastic, 1994.

Joshua's Night Whispers illustrated by Rhonda Mitchell. Orchard Books, 1994.

Julius illustrated by Dav Pilkey. Scholastic, 1993.

Just Like Josh Gibson illustrated by Beth Peck. Simon & Schuster, 2004.

The Leaving Morning illustrated by David Soman. Scholastic, 1992.

Lily Brown's Paintings illustrated by E. B. Lewis. Scholastic, 2006.

Looking for Red. Simon & Schuster, 2002.

Mama Bird, Baby Birds illustrated by Rhonda Mitchell. Orchard Books, 1994.

Maniac Monkeys on Magnolia Street illustrated by John Ward. Random House, 1999.

One of Three illustrated by David Soman. Scholastic, 1991.

On the Fringe edited by Donald R. Gallo. Dial, 2001.

The Other Side: Shorter Poems. Orchard Books, 1998.

Rain Feet illustrated by Rhonda Mitchell. Scholastic, 1994.

The Rolling Store illustrated by Peter Catalanotto. Orchard Books, 1997.

Running Back to Ludie. Orchard Books, 2001.

Shoes Like Miss Alice's illustrated by Ken Page. Orchard Books, 1995.

Songs of Faith. Scholastic, 1998.

A Sweet Smell of Roses illustrated by Eric Velasquez. Simon & Schuster, 2004.

Tell Me a Story, Mama illustrated by David Soman. Orchard Books, 1989.

Toning the Sweep. Scholastic Library Publishing, 1993.

Violet's Music illustrated by Laura Huliska-Beith. Penguin, 2004.

The Wedding illustrated by David Soman. Orchard Books, 1999.

When I Am Old with You illustrated by David Soman. Scholastic, 1990.

When Mules Flew on Magnolia Street illustrated by John Ward. Random House, 2000.

Violet's Music Script

Roles

Caller	Juan	Narrator Three
Angel	Narrator One	Chorus (Three readers)
Randy	Narrator Two	

Narrator One: When Violet was a baby, just a few hours old,

Narrator Two: she banged her rattle against the crib,

Narrator Three: hoping others in the nursery would join in.

Chorus: *Boom … Shake*
Beat … Shake

Narrator One: All day long, Violet played that rattle.

Caller: Could she find other babies to play along?

Angel, Randy, and Juan:
No, she couldn't.

Narrator Two: But she'd keep looking.

Narrator Three: Violet played her music all alone.

Narrator One: On Violet's second birthday Aunt Bertha brought gifts …

Narrator Two: and a box full of paper, crayons, glitter, and glue to make horns that would wail …

Narrator Three: Violet tooted from morning till that night.

Chorus: *WHAH WOO WOO*

Narrator Three: All day long.

Narrator One: She tried to get everyone to toot with her all day.

Chorus: *WHAH WOO WOO*

Narrator Two: Oh yeah. Violet blew that horn.

Caller: Could she get her family to play with her?

Angel, Randy, and Juan:
No, she couldn't.

Narrator Three: But she'd keep on looking. Violet blew her horn all alone.

Narrator One:	Violet wondered in kindergarten if there were other kids like her,
Narrator Two:	who dreamed music, thought music, all day long.
Caller:	But she found that ...
Angel, Randy, and Juan:	some liked to paint, some liked to paste, others liked to play in the sandbox, and still others just liked to stand around eating paste.
Narrator Three:	No one wanted to play music all day long.
Narrator One:	One day at the beach Violet played with a badminton racket,
Narrator Two:	a pretend guitar, hoping someone would join in.
Chorus:	*Plink Plink Pluck Pluck*
Narrator Two:	Violet played guitar.
Caller:	Could she find a fellow guitarist buried in the sand?
Angel, Randy, and Juan:	No, she couldn't.
Narrator Three:	But she'd keep looking. Violet played her guitar all alone.
Caller:	With Violet, you see, it was music all the time.
Angel, Randy, and Juan:	Breakfast time. Dinner time. Bath time. And all times in between.
Narrator One:	Whenever she walked down the street or hid behind the market's vegetable bins,
Narrator Two:	or sat on the fire escape, Violet was always looking for kids like her.
Caller:	Could she find them at the zoo?
Angel, Randy, and Juan:	Nope.
Caller:	At the museum?
Angel, Randy, and Juan:	Too quiet.
Narrator Three:	And forget about the dentist. But she'd keep looking. Violet and her music, always looking.

© 2006 by Toni Buzzeo (UpstartBooks)

Narrator One: Until ...
one day a few summers later,

Narrator Two: Violet was playing her guitar

Angel, Randy, and Juan:
(a real one now)

Narrator Two: in the park.

Chorus: *Twang Twang*
Yeah Yeah
Twang Twang
Yeah!

Narrator Three: When, over by the fountain,
someone started beating a drum ...

Narrator One: Then, behind the jungle gym,
a saxophone blew real smooth ...

Narrator Two: And over beside the flower garden,
someone started to sing ...

Narrator One: Now Angel, Randy, and Juan are in Violet's band.

Narrator Two: And if you ask any of them whether they thought they'd
find each other,

Narrator Three: they'll say:

Angel, Randy, and Juan:
Oh yeah, we did, we knew we would. 'Cause when
we were in the nursery, then were two, and later in
kindergarten and at the beach, we kept on looking
for kids playing music too!

Chorus: *Shake*
TWANG
PLINK
Pluck
WHAH
WOO, YEAH!

The End

Violet's Music Activities

Social Studies Connections

Multiple Intelligences

Howard Gardner is a proponent of the theory of nine distinct intelligences in humans—Visual/Spatial, Verbal/Linguistic, Mathematical/Logical, Bodily/Kinesthetic, Musical/Rhythmic, Interpersonal, Intrapersonal, Naturalist, and Existential. Before beginning this activity and What Kind of Smart Are You? below, familiarize yourself with these nine intelligences. An online overview article with many links entitled "Multiple Intelligences: It's Not How Smart You Are, It's How You're Smart!" by Walter McKenzie is available at www.education-world.com/a_curr/curr207.shtml.

Thomas Armstrong has re-titled the intelligences in kid-friendly language:

- Word Smart (Linguistic Intelligence)

- Number/Reasoning Smart (Logical/Mathematical Intelligence)

- Picture Smart (Spatial Intelligence)

- Body Smart (Bodily/Kinesthetic Intelligence)

- Music Smart (Musical Intelligence)

- People Smart (Interpersonal Intelligence)

- Self Smart (Intrapersonal Intelligence)

- Nature Smart (Naturalist Intelligence)

Others have re-titled the ninth intelligence:

- Wondering Smart (Existential Intelligence)

Students sometimes judge themselves to be "smart" based only on the Verbal/Linguistic and Mathematical/Logical intelligences we have long emphasized in public education. But if we introduce multiple intelligences, every student will know him or herself to be "smart" in one or more dominant intelligence!

After introducing the theory of multiple intelligences to students, ask them to discuss Violet's predominant intelligence. When did she start to exhibit it? Invite students to give examples of it from each stage of her life.

> **Life Skills Standards**
>
> **Self-Regulation**
>
> - Performs self-appraisal
>
> - Maintains a healthy self-concept
>
> **Thinking and Reasoning**
>
> - Understands and applies the basic principles of presenting an argument

What Kind of Smart Are You?

After completing the Multiple Intelligences activity above, invite students to think about their own dominant intelligences. Ask them to use the What Kind of Smart Are You? graphic organizer (page 126) to choose their primary and secondary intelligences and give evidence for it in their class work, accomplishments, and personal pursuits. (A good resource for your own learning is Thomas Armstrong's *Multiple Intelligences in the Classroom, Second Edition* (ASCD, 2000). You can read Chapter 3, "Describing Intelligences in Students" online at www.ascd.org/ed_topics/2000armstrong/chapter3.html.

Now invite students to create small groups (or assign small groups) and analyze the primary and secondary intelligences of each of the other members of their group. Before beginning, engage students in a conversation about looking for each group member's strengths. Ask them to provide evidence that supports their claims. Ask each group to choose a speaker who can present their group findings. This should be an exercise in confidence-building and respect for each individual.

Life Skills Standards

Self-Regulation

- Performs self-appraisal

- Maintains a healthy self concept

Thinking and Reasoning

- Understands and applies the basic principles of presenting an argument

Working with Others

- Displays effective interpersonal communication skills

You've Gotta Have Friends

Throughout *Violet's Music*, Violet searches for other "kids like her." We all seek out those with similar interests and abilities to share the things we enjoy doing. Invite students to reflect on something in their lives they love to do and are talented at.

Then ask them to think about one or two people who share their passions. Ask them to complete the You've Gotta Have Friends Interview Sheet on page 127 by asking these friends some questions. When the interviews are complete, engage students in a group discussion of their findings.

Life Skills Standards

Self-Regulation

- Performs self-appraisal

- Maintains a healthy self concept

Working with Others

- Displays effective interpersonal communication skills

Language Arts Connection
Words and Music

In *Violet's Music*, Angela Johnson uses words to express musical sounds that Violet makes with all sorts of objects and finally with an instrument. Re-read the text with students and undertake a hunt for these "musical words" and the objects Violet uses to make them. Record your findings on the Words and Music graphic organizer on page 128. Be sure that students "read" the illustrations as well as the text. Ask them: What else does Violet make "music" with and what sound words might they use to describe this music?

Language Arts Standards

Reading

- Uses reading skills and strategies to understand and interpret a variety of literary texts

Music Connections

Musical Inspiration

In her interview, Angela Johnson shares information about the many types of music she enjoys, from jazz to Reggae and several specific musicians she likes:

"I love all kinds of music. I am a big fan of jazz. Anything Billie Holiday or Nina Simone sang knocks me out. I grew up on Motown and Rock. But I think the music I love most as an adult is Reggae. Bob Marley, Bunny Wailer ... amazing. I must say though that I'm a big fan of Baroque music also. It's perfect on Sunday mornings."

Share examples of these types of music and from several of these musicians and ask students to discuss how the music might have influenced Johnson in writing *Violet's Music*.

> ### Arts Standards
>
> **Music**
>
> * Knows and applies appropriate criteria to music and music performances

Call and Response

In "call and response" there is an alternation between the leader and a chorus (often the audience). It requires participation of the audience with the performers. Invite students to listen to three "call and response" songs on the America's Story Web site at www.americasstory.com/sh/kid songs/sh_kidsongs_callresp_1.html.

Angela Johnson uses traditional "call and response" techniques in her storytelling in *Violet's Music*. Call students' attention to the instances of "call and response" in the text and the way they play out in the reader's theater of the book, where there is a Caller and a group of responders in Angel, Randy, and Juan.

Because Violet's passion is music, this is a perfect choice in the story, as call and response is an essential characteristic of African music and has become an important element of African American music.

> ### Arts Standards
>
> **Music**
>
> * Understands the relationship between music and history and culture

What Kind of Smart Are You?

WONDERING SMART Does he/she love to ask—and answer—**big** questions like "Why are we here on Earth?"				
NATURE SMART Does he/she love animals, being out in nature, or taking care of the environment?				
PEOPLE SMART Is he/she very good at working with others, organizing groups, and understanding other peoples' ideas?				
SELF SMART Does he/she seem to know him- or herself especially well and is he/she peaceful and confident?				
MUSIC SMART Does he/she love to sing or play an instrument and love music more than anything else?				
BODY SMART Does he/she love to run or dance or play physical games and work hard?				
NUMBER/REASONING SMART Does he/she love numbers, science, computers, and figuring out how things work?				
WORD SMART Does he/she love words, reading, writing, telling stories, speaking and wordplay?				
PICTURE SMART Does he/she love to draw, design, or create beautiful things using photography or building materials?				
Student Name				

You've Gotta Have Friends Interview Sheet

Student Name_____

Friend's Name _____

How old were you when you discovered your interest in/talent for (fill in friend's interest)
_____?

_____

_____

_____

_____

_____

Do you know many other kids who share your interest/passion?

_____

_____

_____

_____

_____

Why do you like to spend time with other kids who share your interest/passion?

_____

_____

_____

_____

_____

 # Words and Music

Object	Sound Words
Rattle	Boom Shake Beat Shake